Gastric Bypass Cookbook: Quick & Easy, Mouthwatering Recipes Tailored for Your New Stomach. Embrace Our 8-Week Bariatric Meal Plan to Tackle Food Addiction and Weight Regain Head-on after Surgery

1st Edition

ISBN: 978-1-916825-10-9

Sites:
Company: mindsparkpressltd.com
Author: meganrushrecipes.com

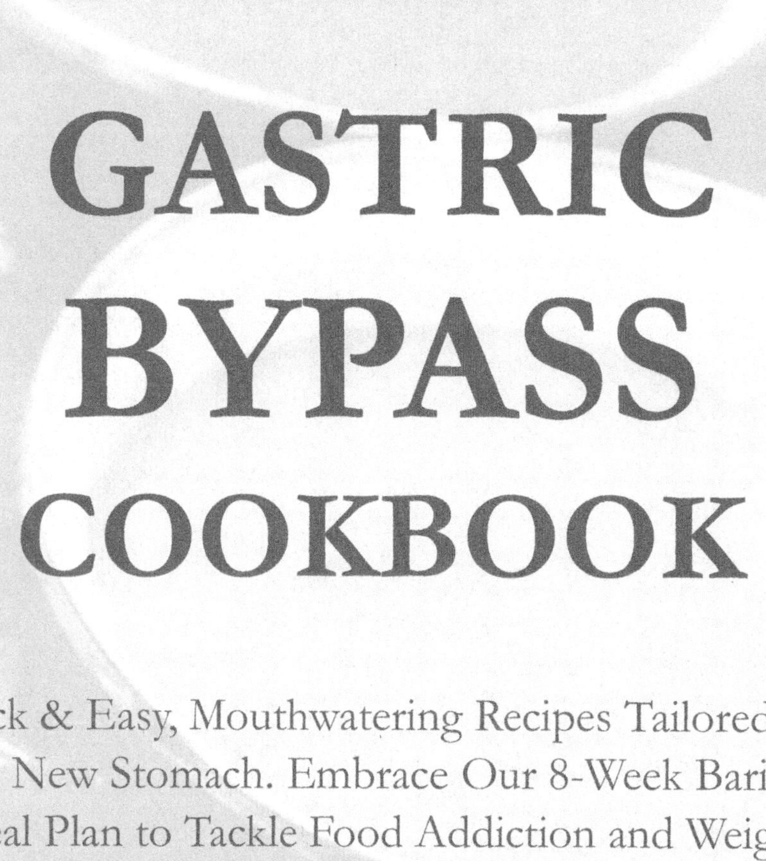

GASTRIC BYPASS COOKBOOK

Quick & Easy, Mouthwatering Recipes Tailored for Your New Stomach. Embrace Our 8-Week Bariatric Meal Plan to Tackle Food Addiction and Weight Regain Head-on after Surgery

MEGAN RUSH

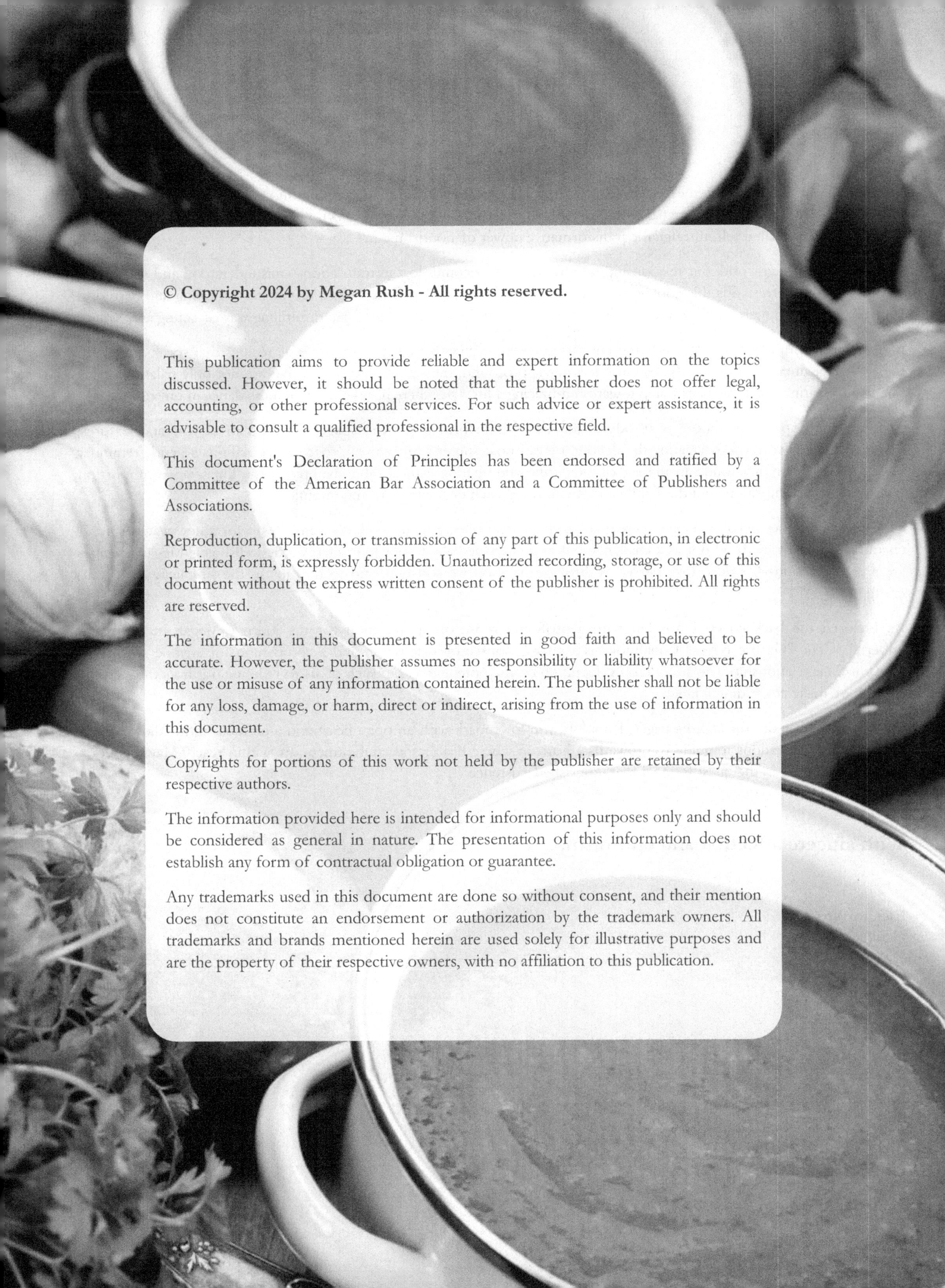

PREFACTION

"Embarking on the pages of the "Gastric Bypass Cookbook," I found myself stepping into a sanctuary of renewal and rediscovery. This masterpiece, curated with passion and precision, is not just a collection of recipes; it's a beacon guiding us toward a rejuvenated self, through the transformative power of nourishment.

In today's fast-paced world, our relationship with food often becomes lost in translation—misunderstood and sometimes mistreated. Yet, here stands this cookbook, crafted by the visionary Megan Rush, as a testament to healing and harmony. It offers more than mere meals; it presents a pathway to embracing a more mindful and fulfilling way of eating and living.

Megan Rush, with her eloquent touch and culinary acumen, brings to us a treasure trove of recipes that speak directly to the soul. Her understanding of the bariatric journey is profound, translating into dishes that are not only palate-pleasing but also nurturing. Each recipe is a step towards embracing a lifestyle where health and happiness dance in unison.

The "Gastric Bypass Cookbook" is an ode to the art of transformation—each page, a melody of flavors and textures, designed to cater to those navigating the delicate phases post-surgery. Megan's approach to cooking is a gentle reminder of the joy and serenity found in the act of preparing and sharing a meal. She champions the importance of portion control, balanced nutrition, and the significance of infusing each dish with care and intention.

This cookbook goes beyond being a mere guide to post-gastric bypass nutrition; it's a manifesto for a new way of life. It encourages us to view food not as a challenge but as a cherished ally in our journey towards well-being. Megan's recipes are a call to action—a call to love ourselves through the food we consume and to find joy in the simplicity of a well-crafted dish.

As I closed the back cover, I was left with a profound sense of appreciation for the journey Megan invites us to undertake. The "Gastric Bypass Cookbook" is a gift—a source of inspiration and a companion for anyone seeking to reinvent their relationship with food. It's a celebration of the potential within each of us to redefine our lives through the choices we make at the dining table.

To those who wander through its pages, I implore you to embark with an open heart and a curious spirit. Allow Megan Rush's culinary creations to guide you towards a horizon where health and contentment are within reach. May this book be your lighthouse in the quest for a vibrant, nourished existence."

With sincere affection and optimism,

Eleanor Voss

Table of Contents

Introduction

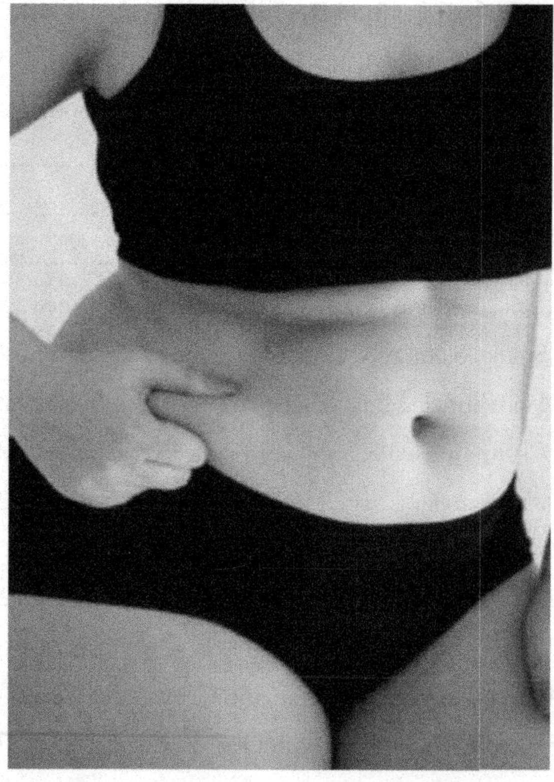

If you have been battling severe obesity and find it difficult to shed weight, your healthcare provider may suggest bariatric surgery. Known as weight reduction surgery, this method is a proven way to lose weight and decrease the risk of several health issues linked to obesity, such as heart disease, high blood pressure, arthritis, stroke, diabetes, and sleep apnea. Bariatric and metabolic surgery refer to the same weight loss procedures, highlighting their effects on both weight and metabolic health. This surgery involves altering your stomach and small intestine, which changes the way your body handles food.

Gastric bypass surgery, a type of bariatric procedure, aids weight loss through multiple mechanisms:

- It decreases the size of your stomach, which leads to consuming fewer calories.
- It alters gut hormones, enhancing satiety and reducing hunger.
- It can address metabolic syndrome associated with obesity. These surgeries are especially beneficial for controlling obesity-related conditions like diabetes, high blood pressure, sleep apnea, and elevated cholesterol levels. They can also avert future health issues. Patients can look forward to an improved quality of life and longer lifespan, thanks to the significant benefits.

Metabolic and bariatric surgeries have advanced over time and are among the most thoroughly researched interventions in contemporary medicine. These surgeries are performed using minimally invasive techniques, including laparoscopic and robotic methods. Such innovations result in less pain, fewer complications, reduced hospital stays, and faster recovery for patients. Their safety profile is on par with, or even surpasses, that of other routine surgeries, such as hip replacements, gallbladder removal, or hysterectomies. Post-surgery, there's a decrease in the absorption of calories, vitamins, and nutrients, making it essential for patients to follow a regimen of prescribed vitamins and nutrient supplements.

Possible complications from the surgery include blood clots, internal bleeding, infections, and issues with the anastomosis—the newly formed connection between the intestines and stomach. A significant concern is the potential leak of digestive fluids and partially digested food through an anastomosis that hasn't healed properly. However, by maintaining a balanced diet, adhering to vitamin requirements, and regular physical activity, patients can achieve lasting weight loss and maintain a healthy digestive system. Dedication and persistence are key to long-term success.

Gastric Bypass Surgery

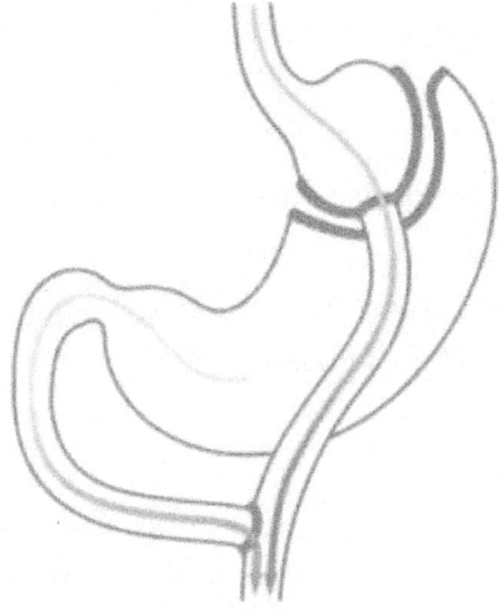

Gastric bypass stands as a prominent option in weight-loss surgeries. In this technique, the upper portion of the stomach is converted into a tiny pouch. This pouch is then linked to the small intestine, establishing a direct path that bypasses the majority of the stomach. Another connection is made further along the small intestine to ensure proper digestive flow. This configuration allows food to skip the majority of the stomach, leading to reduced calorie absorption and quicker satiety after meals.

Healthcare professionals may recommend gastric bypass to patients with a Body Mass Index (BMI) of over 40, or for those with a BMI over 35 who also suffer from serious health issues related to their weight. A BMI above 40 usually indicates an excess weight of at least 100 pounds.

Roux-en-Y Gastric Bypass Overview

The Roux-en-Y gastric bypass, often simply referred to as gastric bypass, has been a cornerstone in bariatric surgery for more than fifty years, with its minimally invasive laparoscopic approach being introduced in 1993. Esteemed for its efficacy in tackling obesity and related health conditions, the procedure is named for its distinctive Y-shaped arrangement.

Procedure Details

- The procedure involves creating a small pouch from the upper portion of the stomach and connecting it directly to the small intestine, effectively bypassing a large part of the stomach.
- The reconfiguration allows food to bypass the main stomach area and the initial part of the small intestine, where it would normally mix with digestive enzymes and stomach acids.
- Surgeons make 4-6 tiny incisions in the abdomen to insert surgical instruments and a camera, which transmits images to a monitor to guide the surgery.

Laparoscopic Surgery Advantages:

- Reduced recovery time and shorter hospital stays
- Lowered pain levels post-surgery
- Less scarring and a decreased risk of post-operative complications such as infections or hernias
- The surgery typically lasts between 2 to 4 hours

Mechanism of Action

By creating a smaller stomach pouch and rerouting the digestive path, gastric bypass restricts how much food can be eaten and decreases calorie absorption. This leads to significant changes in hormones related to hunger and metabolism, impacting appetite and metabolic functions. The surgery can show metabolic health improvements, like reversing type 2 diabetes, even before significant weight loss occurs. It also offers quick relief from acid reflux symptoms. Post-operative care includes following a nutritious diet, avoiding NSAIDs such as ibuprofen, and refraining from smoking.

Considering Gastric Bypass

Advantages:

- Quick initial reduction in weight, with patients often losing 60-80% of their excess weight early on
- Durable results, with many patients keeping off over 50% of their excess weight for up to 20 years after surgery
- Proven effectiveness in addressing health issues linked to obesity

Disadvantages:

- Higher risk of complications compared to procedures like the sleeve gastrectomy
- Post-operative restrictions on NSAID use
- A lifelong necessity for nutritional supplements to avoid deficiencies in vitamins and minerals such as B12, iron, folate, and calcium

Patients may achieve a 70% or greater reduction in excess weight over time, with the actual amount depending on surgical details and lifestyle changes. Gastric bypass can significantly improve or even resolve conditions related to obesity, including acid reflux, high blood pressure, elevated cholesterol levels, sleep apnea, infertility, heart disease, diabetes, and stroke risk, fostering a more vibrant and active life.

Should weight loss goals not be met, or if weight is regained, alternative strategies are available. Maintaining the desired outcomes requires lifestyle adjustments and regular follow-ups with healthcare providers.

Potential Complications:

- More complex than other bariatric procedures, such as the sleeve gastrectomy
- Risk of nutritional deficiencies
- Possibilities of bowel obstructions and other surgical complications
- Increased risk of ulcers, particularly for individuals who smoke or use NSAIDs
- Risk of "dumping syndrome," characterized by discomfort when eating or drinking too quickly, especially sugary foods or drinks.

Pre-Operative Evaluation

Prior to your gastric bypass surgery, you will visit a specialized clinic for an extensive assessment to verify if you are a suitable candidate for the procedure. This comprehensive evaluation will cover:

- **Physical Condition**: Employing methods such as blood tests, imaging, and X-rays to evaluate your general health status.
- **Eating Behaviors**: A review of your dietary habits and food preferences.
- **Psychological Health**: Discussion around your goals for undergoing surgery, any present psychological concerns, and your preparedness for the profound lifestyle adjustments following the operation.

To enhance the safety and success rate of the operation, you may be recommended to follow a restricted-calorie diet in the weeks leading up to the surgery to potentially decrease the size of your liver.

Pre-Surgical Preparations

In preparation for your surgery, you will undergo a series of evaluations and consultations:

- **Medical Assessments**: Including a thorough physical examination, an ultrasound of the gallbladder if necessary, blood work, and other pertinent evaluations to confirm your surgical readiness.
- **Consultations with Your Doctor**: To ensure any chronic conditions you may have, such as high blood pressure, lung problems, or diabetes, are under control.
- **Nutritional Guidance**: Providing you with detailed information about the diet you'll need to follow.
- **Informative Sessions**: Offering a deeper understanding of the surgical process, what to expect after surgery, and the potential risks and complications involved.
- **Psychological Support**: Assessing your mental and emotional preparedness for undergoing the surgery and the significant lifestyle changes thereafter.

Extra Measures:

- Smokers are strongly advised to quit several weeks prior to the operation as smoking can hinder the healing process and elevate the risk of complications.
- Disclose all substances you are taking to your surgeon, including over-the-counter medications, vitamins, supplements, or herbal remedies.
- If you suspect you could be pregnant, inform your surgeon at once.
- Certain medications that may interfere with blood clotting, such as ibuprofen, warfarin, and aspirin, might need to be temporarily stopped; always check with your healthcare provider before making any changes to your medication regimen.
- Prepare your living space to accommodate your recovery needs post-surgery.
- Follow specific instructions about eating and drinking on the eve of your operation.
- If instructed, take only the medications deemed essential with a small sip of water on the morning of your operation.
- Arrive on time at the hospital on the day designated for your surgery.

Post-Operative Recovery Process

Following your gastric bypass procedure in the hospital, you can expect a stay ranging from one to two days, depending on how quickly you recover.

Recovery Phase After Surgery:

- Patients typically spend between one and four days in the hospital after the operation.
- On the day of the surgery, you'll be encouraged to sit up and move around a bit.
- A nasal catheter may be inserted for the first one to two days to help remove stomach fluids.
- A catheter for urine drainage may also be utilized.
- Initially, you will be on a restricted diet, starting with liquids and gradually moving to pureed or soft foods over the first one to three days.
- In some cases, a tube may be placed into the section of the stomach that was bypassed to allow fluids to drain.
- You might wear special stockings to help prevent the formation of blood clots in your legs.
- Preventative measures against blood clots may also include the use of medication injections.
- Pain management will be provided, which can be administered orally or through IV.

Discharge typically occurs once you can ingest liquid or pureed food without issues and can move around with manageable pain. Following post-operative instructions is crucial. The first year post-surgery sees the most significant weight loss, with patients often losing between 10 to 20 pounds per month, tapering off as time progresses. The greatest reduction in weight, frequently exceeding half of the excess body weight, is usually achieved within the first two years. This substantial weight loss can lead to improvements in various health conditions, and most patients report an enhanced ease in performing daily tasks and improved mobility.

Surgical Process

Initially, patients are given a general anesthesia to ensure they stay asleep and pain-free during the operation.

Surgical Procedure Overview:

- The approach to gastric bypass surgery is tailored to meet the specific requirements of the patient and the preferred technique of the surgeon.
- While some procedures may require larger abdominal incisions, the vast majority are performed laparoscopically, entailing several minor cuts.
- Utilizing either the open or laparoscopic technique, the surgeon creates a small stomach pouch from the upper section of the stomach, limiting its capacity to approximately 1 oz. of food, compared to the normal stomach capacity of about 3 quarts.
- Subsequently, the surgeon connects a part of the small intestine directly to the newly formed stomach pouch. This arrangement skips the larger part of the stomach and the beginning of the small intestine, directing food straight to the mid-section of the small intestine.
- Typically, the operation takes a few hours to complete. Afterwards, patients are moved to a recovery area, where medical staff closely monitor them for any signs of complications.

Post-Operative Dietary and Weight Loss Expectations

Following gastric bypass surgery, your initial diet will consist of small quantities of soft foods and liquids for the first month. As you progress, you will gradually reintroduce solid foods into your diet. You will notice a sensation of fullness after eating only about two teaspoons of food. To compensate for potential nutritional deficiencies, your physician may advise taking dietary supplements.

In the first two years following the surgery, most individuals typically lose between 50% to 66% of their surplus body weight. Weight reduction is usually ongoing for about 18 months before it plateaus.

Gastric bypass surgery, like any significant surgical procedure, entails certain risks, both immediate and long-term, that are common to abdominal operations:

Common Risks Include:

- Infection risks
- Negative reactions to anesthesia
- Respiratory issues
- Leaks in the gastrointestinal tract
- Significant bleeding
- Formation of blood clots

Specific Risks Associated with the Procedure:

- Enlargement of the stomach pouch, which might stretch back to its pre-surgery size over time.
- Separation along the staple line if the staples become loose.
- Nutritional deficits due to the body's adjusted ability to absorb vital nutrients.
- Stomal stenosis, which is a narrowing of the opening between the stomach and the small intestine, leading to vomiting, acid reflux, or, in extreme cases, difficulty eating.
- Dumping syndrome occurs when food moves from the stomach to the small intestine too quickly, causing symptoms such as dizziness, sweating, nausea, light-headedness, and possibly diarrhea or severe tiredness.
- Formation of gallstones as a result of quick weight loss, although medication can mitigate this issue.

Given the surgery's impact on the digestion and absorption of food, ongoing medical evaluations are crucial to monitor and manage nutrient levels effectively.

Long-term Complications May Include:

- Hernias
- Gastric perforations
- Intestinal blockages
- Ulcers
- Gallstones
- Dumping syndrome with symptoms like vomiting, diarrhea, or nausea
- Low blood sugar levels (hypoglycemia)
- Vomiting
- Risk of malnutrition

While these potential complications are a cause for concern, they are infrequent and generally manageable with proper medical attention. In very rare cases, they could lead to life-threatening conditions. Being informed about these risks and maintaining close communication with your healthcare team is critical for your recovery and long-term health.

Risk of Nutritional Deficiencies

Following bariatric surgery, there's an altered capacity for the body to adequately absorb essential vitamins and minerals, heightening the likelihood of nutritional deficiencies. Signs of such deficiencies can include enduring exhaustion, difficulty breathing, rapid heartbeat, a pale appearance, numbness or tingling sensations, and overall weakness. While adopting a well-rounded diet can alleviate some of these issues, it's common for patients to require ongoing supplementation with vitamins and minerals after surgery. Routine blood screenings will be essential to identify and remedy any deficiencies that may arise.

Potential for Gastrointestinal Leakage

After undergoing gastric bypass, there's a risk that food could leak into the abdominal cavity, leading to serious infections. Warning signs of a gastrointestinal leak encompass high fever, rapid heart rate, abdominal discomfort, shivering, and quickened breathing rates. Experiencing any of these symptoms warrants urgent medical care. Treatment for such a condition may involve additional surgery and antibiotic therapy.

Excess Skin Following Significant Weight Loss

The rapid weight loss that occurs after bariatric surgery often results in surplus skin, particularly around the abdomen, breasts, arms, and hips. Procedures such as abdominoplasty (tummy tuck) can help remove this excess skin, though they are typically considered cosmetic surgeries. If you're considering such post-weight loss surgeries, it's important to discuss with your healthcare provider to understand the options and timing for these procedures based on your health and recovery progress.

Blood Clot Prevention and Management

Following surgery, preventive strategies are employed to minimize the risk of blood clots. These can include the use of compression garments or the administration of blood-thinning medications. Despite these precautions, there's still a possibility for clots to form, often in the veins of the lower legs or, more seriously, in the lungs—a condition known as pulmonary embolism. Symptoms indicative of a blood clot include leg pain, redness, swelling, or a warm feeling in the affected area, alongside sudden chest pain, difficulty breathing, unexplained coughing (possibly with blood), lightheadedness, or fainting. Encountering any of these symptoms necessitates urgent medical intervention.

Risk of Infection at the Surgical Site

Infections at the site of surgical incisions pose a common risk during the healing process. Signs that an infection may have developed include increased pain, redness, warmth at the site, swelling, or pus discharge from the incision. Prompt medical evaluation is critical, and treatment often involves antibiotics.

Emphasizing the importance of closely following post-surgical care instructions can significantly lower these risks, but it's important to acknowledge that complications can still occur. Engaging in an open dialogue with your healthcare provider to fully understand these potential risks, their signs, and the appropriate responses is crucial prior to deciding on undergoing gastric bypass surgery.

Bariatric Diet and Post-Operative Care

The journey through bariatric surgery includes adopting a revamped dietary approach aimed at fostering successful weight management and enhancing overall wellness.

Dietary Recommendations Post-Surgery:

- Emphasize meals rich in essential nutrients while maintaining a diet that's low in calories, fats, and sugars.
- Vigilant monitoring of portion sizes, calorie consumption, and protein intake is crucial.
- Adopt a mindful eating practice, ensuring food is chewed to a fine consistency to facilitate digestion.
- Initially, it's advisable to limit the consumption of fibrous grains, raw vegetables, and certain meats, opting instead for more digestible forms such as minced or ground meat.
- Avoid behaviors that may lead to gas accumulation, such as chewing ice, drinking through straws, or ingesting fizzy beverages.
- Steer clear of foods high in sugar content, including sweets and sugary drinks, to prevent dumping syndrome and other complications.
- Post-operative caloric intake should start from a range of 300-600 calories per day with a gradual increase, keeping the upper limit to no more than 1,000 calories daily during the initial recovery phase.

These guidelines are designed to aid in the recovery process, ensuring the stomach adjusts properly while minimizing the risk of complications. It's also essential for patients to stay hydrated, consuming enough fluids between meals to support their nutritional needs without overfilling their reduced stomach capacity.

Hydration and Dietary Adjustments Post-Bariatric Surgery

Maintaining proper hydration is paramount after bariatric surgery:

- It's essential to drink plenty of fluids between meals, avoiding caffeine, to prevent dehydration.
- Strive for at least 64 ounces (about 8 cups) of water or other non-caffeinated fluids daily.
- Alcohol should be avoided as its absorption rate increases after surgery, potentially leading to unexpected levels of intoxication.

Protein Intake's Role

Protein is vital for maintaining muscle mass. Include high-quality protein sources in your diet, such as lean meats, fish, poultry, eggs, dairy, tofu, and soy products. Aim for a protein goal of 65-75 grams per day, relying on liquid or soft protein supplements in the initial stages post-surgery.

Supplemental Nutrition Due to changes in the digestive system post-surgery, absorption of nutrients may be reduced. Adherence to prescribed vitamin and mineral supplements is crucial. Modify solid supplements into crushed or liquid forms for enhanced absorption.

Cautious Consumption

Some foods and drinks may irritate the stomach or hinder recovery post-surgery:

- Steer clear of caffeinated and carbonated beverages for the first three months.
- Postpone alcohol consumption for at least six months following the procedure.
- Avoid digestion-challenging foods such as dry meats, spicy foods, fatty meals, and certain sugar alcohols.
- To prevent dumping syndrome—characterized by rapid gastric emptying that causes nausea and discomfort—avoid high-sugar foods, eat slowly, and chew food thoroughly.
- Restrict intake of foods that are difficult to digest, including certain meats, whole grains, shellfish, and specific vegetables and fruits.

Diet Before Surgery

In preparation for surgery, follow a 1-2 week diet focusing on:

- Meal replacement drinks or high-protein shakes.
- Sugar-free liquids (artificial sweeteners permitted).
- Clear soup broths.
- Vegetable juices, such as V8.
- Soft cereals, like cream of wheat or rice.
- A limited amount of lean meats and vegetables as advised by your healthcare professional. Ensure a gap of at least 30 minutes between eating and drinking to practice the separation of solids and liquids, preparing for post-surgery nutrition.

In essence, bariatric surgery necessitates a deep commitment to changing dietary habits and lifestyle. Work closely with your medical team to tailor your diet and ensure a successful recovery and optimal long-term health outcomes.

Post-Operative Diet and Stages

Navigating the post-operative diet after bariatric surgery is pivotal for ensuring smooth recovery and maximizing health benefits. This dietary journey is meticulously structured into stages to gradually reintegrate your system to a new way of eating while prioritizing protein intake for healing and muscle maintenance.

Essential Protein Sources for Recovery:

- **Seafood:** Incorporate fatty fish like salmon and lean options such as tilapia for their high-quality protein and omega-3 fatty acids.
- **Poultry:** Chicken breasts provide a lean protein source that's versatile for meal preparation.
- **Lean Beef:** Select cuts like sirloin to fulfill protein needs without excessive fat.
- **Legumes:** Lentils and beans are excellent for plant-based protein, enriching your diet with fiber.
- **Eggs:** Highly nutritious, offering a complete protein source, ideal in any form—boiled, scrambled, or as part of a dish.
- **Dairy:** Greek yogurt and low-fat cheese offer calcium and protein, supporting bone health.
- **Tofu and Tempeh:** Soy products are a great alternative for those looking for plant-based protein options.
- **Nuts and Seeds:** In moderation, they provide protein along with healthy fats, though they should be consumed cautiously due to their high-calorie content.

Dietary Phases Post-Surgery:

- **Initial Phase - Clear Liquids:** Start with broths, clear fruit juices, and sugar-free gelatin to maintain hydration without straining the stomach.
- **Second Phase - Pureed Foods and Full Liquids:** Gradually introduce thicker liquids and pureed foods, such as smooth soups and pureed fruits, to increase nutrient intake.
- **Third Phase - Soft Foods:** Add semi-solid foods that are easier to digest, like soft-cooked eggs, flaky fish, and tender legumes, to the diet.
- **Final Phase - Solid Foods:** Transition to a more standard diet, focusing on small, well-chewed bites of solid foods rich in protein, alongside healthy fats and fibers.

It's critical to proceed through these stages under the guidance of a healthcare professional to ensure each phase is nutritionally adequate and to adjust based on individual tolerance and recovery progress.

The 5-Day Pouch Reset - Rekindling Your Weight Loss Journey

If you're experiencing a plateau in your weight loss journey after gastric bypass surgery, or if you find your appetite control and food choices slipping, the 5-Day Pouch Reset could offer a much-needed kickstart.

Understanding the 5-Day Pouch Reset: This regimen is aimed at recalibrating your body's response to food by focusing on a protein-rich diet that controls intake, essentially hitting the "reset button" on your gastric pouch. It's designed to help you redevelop healthy eating habits and enhance your sense of satiety.

Indications for the Reset

You might consider the **5-Day Pouch Reset** if you:

- Have hit a weight loss plateau.
- Are seeing gradual weight increases.
- Notice a lapse in managing your food portions.
- Wish to regain control over your dietary habits.

Plan Overview for the 5-Day Pouch Reset

Days 1 & 2 - Focus on Liquid Protein

The initial two days revolve around consuming liquid protein supplements to kickstart the reset process, including:

- Soups enriched with protein, serving as your main meal base.
- Protein-infused smoothies, acting as nutritious snacks to keep you hydrated and nourished.

Days 3 to 5 - Introducing Solid Proteins

The latter part of the reset introduces a mix of liquid and solid protein sources to maintain fullness and transition smoothly back to a regular diet.

- Continue with the protein-rich soups and smoothies.
- Add in solid protein options such as protein bars or snacks to extend satiety and provide consistent energy.
- Target a daily protein goal of 90 grams while maintaining a controlled calorie count.

After the Reset

Completing the 5-Day Pouch Reset should make it easier to return to a balanced, nutritious diet. While relying on protein supplements can be helpful, they should complement, not replace, a varied diet. Consultation with a nutritionist or healthcare professional is advisable to tailor dietary choices to your specific health objectives and ensure a successful weight loss journey continuation.

Incorporating Exercise into Your Post-Surgery Lifestyle

After undergoing weight reduction surgery, embracing physical activity is as vital as adhering to the new dietary recommendations for a comprehensive recovery and maintaining long-term weight loss success.

Advantages of Engaging in Post-Surgery Exercise:

1. **Promotes Healthy Circulation**: Regular physical activity enhances blood flow, crucial for delivering oxygen and nutrients throughout the body.
2. **Minimizes Blood Clot Risks**: Being active helps in preventing the formation of blood clots, a significant post-operative concern.
3. **Aids in Digestive Health**: Exercise plays a key role in facilitating consistent bowel movements, addressing post-surgical digestive changes.
4. **Accelerates Healing**: The boost in circulation from exercise can lead to quicker healing of surgical sites.

Developing an Effective Exercise Regimen:

1. **Initial Steps**: Start with gentle activities such as walking soon after your operation. Opt for shorter, frequent strolls to build stamina without overexertion.

2. **Progressive Increase**: Patients who have had minimally invasive surgery can usually resume normal activities within 2-4 weeks, while those who had open surgery might need up to twelve weeks for the same. It's crucial to pace yourself and heed your body's signals.

3. **Customized Exercise Plans**:
   - **Goal Setting**: Clearly outline your fitness objectives, ensuring they are practical and within reach.
   - **Variety in Exercises**: Mix up your workout routines to maintain interest and challenge different muscle groups.
   - **Pursue Enjoyable Activities:** Consistency is more likely when you're doing exercises you enjoy, such as swimming, yoga, or biking.
   - **Integrate Exercise into Daily Routines**: Simple lifestyle changes, like using stairs instead of elevators, can significantly increase your daily activity levels.

4. **Tips for Maintaining Regular Activity**:
   - **Identify Your Prime Time**: Exercise when you feel most energetic and motivated.
   - **Be Prepared**: Keep exercise attire accessible to eliminate excuses.
   - **Set Step Goals**: Aiming for a daily step count, like 10,000 steps, provides a clear target and motivation.
   - **Mind Your Meals**: Wait for about two hours after eating before engaging in physical activity to avoid gastrointestinal discomfort.

- **Allow for Recovery**: Rest days are essential for muscle repair and growth after intense workouts.

5. **Importance of Hydration**: Staying hydrated is paramount, especially with a smaller stomach capacity. Drink water regularly throughout the day to prevent dehydration and mistakenly interpreting thirst for hunger.

Beginning an exercise routine post-weight reduction surgery is a personal journey that varies from one individual to another. Engage closely with your healthcare providers, set achievable goals, and most importantly, tune into your body's needs and limits.

Integrating Exercise into Post-Surgery Recovery

After bariatric surgery, it's essential to incorporate physical activity gradually into your routine, emphasizing low-impact exercises to ensure both safety and effectiveness. Here's a tailored exercise regimen for individuals recovering from weight reduction surgery:

1. **Strolls**:
    - **What**: Walking is the most straightforward yet highly recommended post-operative physical activity.
    - **How**: Begin with leisurely short walks, progressively extending your walking time as you gain stamina. Maintain good posture and active arm movements for additional upper body engagement.

2. **Static Leg Raises**:
    - **What**: Aims to strengthen leg muscles without putting pressure on the abdominal region.
    - **How**: Lie flat on your back and lift each leg slowly off the ground, holding the position briefly before switching legs.

3. **Chair-Based Marching**:
    - **What**: An effective exercise for engaging lower abdominal muscles and legs gently.
    - **How**: Sit upright on a chair and alternately lift your knees towards the chest, mimicking a marching motion.

4. **Arm Rotations**:
    - **What**: Boosts upper body strength and flexibility.
    - **How**: With arms extended to the sides, rotate them in small to large circles, then reverse the direction.

5. **Modified Squats**:
    - **What**: Enhances the strength of thigh and buttock muscles.

- **How**: Stand with feet apart, lower your body by bending the knees (without extending past toes), and then rise back up.

6. **Seated Knee Extensions**:
    - **What**: Focuses on the quadriceps without stressing the joints excessively.
    - **How**: Sit with feet flat on the floor, then extend one leg at a time, hold, and alternate.

7. **Breathing Exercises**:
    - **What**: Improves lung function and promotes relaxation.
    - **How**: In a comfortable seated or lying position, deeply inhale through the nose and exhale slowly through the mouth.

8. **Adaptive Yoga**:
    - **What**: Incorporates gentle yoga poses done with the aid of a chair for increased flexibility and stress reduction.
    - **How**: Engage in poses like the seated cat-cow stretch or spinal twists, following guides or classes tailored for chair yoga.

9. **Resistance Training**:
    - **What**: Uses bands to offer strength training without heavy weights.
    - **How**: Perform exercises like bicep curls and leg presses, ensuring proper resistance levels and form.

10. **Aquatic Exercises**:
    - **What**: Full-body workout in water, ideal for reducing joint strain.
    - **How**: Once healing is complete, swimming or joining water aerobics classes can provide low-impact resistance training.

Before starting any exercise plan post-surgery, it's vital to consult with your healthcare team. They can offer personalized advice based on your recovery progress and overall health status, ensuring your exercise regimen supports your healing and weight loss goals effectively.

Initiating Post-Surgery Nutrition: The Clear Liquid Diet

The initial phase after bariatric surgery is critical for recovery, emphasizing the need for a gentle reintroduction to eating. This early post-operative period is dedicated to the clear liquid diet, marking the first stage of your nutritional progression.

Length and Objectives

This diet commences on the day following surgery and is typically maintained for 1 to 3 weeks. Its purpose extends beyond merely ensuring the stomach can manage intake; it's designed to pave the way for a gradual reintegration of more varied foods into your meal plan.

Consumption Guidelines

Patients are encouraged to consume 3 oz. of clear liquids every half hour. Though this might seem challenging at first due to post-surgery discomfort, it's important to stick with it as it becomes easier over time. To avoid introducing air into the stomach, which can cause gas and bloating, it's important to drink slowly and avoid using straws or chewing gum.

Recommended Liquids

The following beverages are suitable for this stage:

- **Watered-Down Apple Juice**: This provides a gentle, hydrating option that's easy on the stomach.
- **Electrolyte-Freezing Pops**: A tasty way to replenish electrolytes and stay hydrated.
- **Lemon-Infused Water**: Offers a refreshing twist and may aid in digestion.
- **Sugar-Free Gelatin with a Citrus Twist**: Adds some variety to your liquid intake without adding sugar.

Incorporating Protein

Adding protein to your clear liquid diet is crucial for supporting tissue repair and maintaining muscle mass. A diluted protein shake, mixed half-and-half with water, offers a balanced way to include protein without overwhelming your system.

Items to Exclude from Your Post-Surgery Diet

After bariatric surgery, certain substances should be avoided to ensure a smooth recovery and effective weight loss journey:

- **Sugar**: Consuming sugar can cause "Dumping Syndrome," characterized by rapid digestion leading to symptoms like severe nausea, diarrhea, and vomiting. Sugary beverages also contribute unnecessary calories, undermining weight loss efforts.
- **Caffeine**: Caffeine can dehydrate the body and exacerbate acid reflux. It's advisable to avoid caffeinated drinks to prevent these issues.
- **Carbonated Beverages**: Any form of carbonated drink, regardless of sugar content, can induce gas and bloating. It's best to steer clear of these both immediately after surgery and as a long-term dietary guideline.

The Importance of Staying Hydrated

Maintaining hydration is crucial for recovery and overall health. Aim to consume between 48 and 64 ounces of water daily. If you find it challenging to meet your hydration needs, consider consulting with your healthcare provider for recommendations on low-calorie electrolyte supplements to help maintain balance.

Expanding Your Clear Liquid Options

As you become more comfortable with your liquid intake, consider incorporating a variety of clear liquids to keep your palate interested and meet your nutritional needs:

- **Herbal Teas**: Opt for unsweetened traditional or fruity herbal teas.
- **Pure Water**: The most reliable source of hydration.
- **Sugar-Free Alternatives**: Look for no-sugar-added popsicles, gelatins, and other refreshments for variety.
- **Clear Broths**: These offer a savory choice that is easy on the digestive system.
- **Decaf Coffee**: A good option for those who miss their regular coffee routine.
- **Diluted Whey Protein Drinks**: Fruit-flavored whey protein can be a good source of protein; just be sure to dilute it with water for better tolerance.

During this initial stage, the focus is on ensuring a smooth healing process, staying hydrated, and introducing gentle nutrition back into your diet. Always engage with your dietitian or medical provider to make informed choices during this critical recovery period.

Stage 1 – Recipes

1. Savory Poultry Broth Recipe

Skill Level: ★★☆☆☆

Prep Duration: 15 mins

Cook Duration: 1 hr 45 mins

Yield: 8 serving

Ingredients:

- 1 small chicken (about 2.5 pounds), chosen for its tender meat
- A dash of ground white pepper for seasoning
- Natural salt, adjusted to your taste
- A sprinkle of garlic powder for an aromatic depth

Directions:

1. Place the chicken in a large pot, covering it completely with water to ensure even cooking and a rich broth.
2. Season the water with a careful addition of ground white pepper, natural salt, and a sprinkle of garlic powder, creating a flavorful base that will infuse the chicken as it cooks.
3. Heat the pot over medium-high until the water boils, then reduce the heat to maintain a gentle simmer. During this time, diligently skim off any foam or impurities that rise to the surface, ensuring a clear broth.
4. After the broth has simmered and the chicken is fully cooked, transfer the pot to the refrigerator to cool for about 1 hour. This chilling step allows the fat to solidify at the top, making it easier to remove and discard, resulting in a leaner broth.
5. Reheat the broth gently before serving, straining if desired for clarity. Any unused broth can be stored for future use, serving as a versatile base for soups, sauces, or other culinary creations.

Nutrition Per Serving:

Kcal 80 | Sodium: 60mg | Protein: 10g | Carbohydrates: 0g | Fat: 4g | Potassium: 75mg

This method of preparing poultry broth emphasizes simplicity and flavor, utilizing minimal seasoning to enhance the natural taste of the chicken. The resulting broth is both nourishing and versatile, ready to be enjoyed on its own or as a foundational component in a variety of dishes.

2. Country Vegetable Essence

Skill Level: ★☆☆☆☆

Prep Duration: 25 mins

Cook Duration: 30 mins

Yield: 4 serving

Ingredients:

- 2.5 oz. carrots, coarsely chopped for a sweet base
- 5.5 cups of water, the foundation of this aromatic broth
- 4 oz. zucchini, thinly sliced for a delicate texture

- 4 oz. leeks, thinly sliced, adding a mild onion-like flavor
- 3 no-salt vegetable bouillon cubes, for a rich, savory depth
- A dash each of rosemary, thyme, oregano, and marjoram, for a herbal bouquet
- A pinch of lavender flowers (optional), for a subtle floral note

Directions:

1. Begin by bringing the water to a gentle boil in a large pot. Dissolve the vegetable bouillon cubes thoroughly to create a flavorful base.
2. Add the chopped carrots, zucchini, and leeks into the simmering broth, introducing a variety of textures and flavors to the mix.
3. Season with rosemary, thyme, oregano, and marjoram, sprinkling in lavender flowers if using. Allow the herbs to simmer gently, infusing the broth with their distinctive flavors for about 25 minutes, creating a harmonious blend.
4. Carefully strain the broth to remove the solids, capturing the essence of the vegetables and herbs in a clear, flavorful liquid.
5. Let the broth cool slightly to enhance its flavors. Serve this comforting, aromatic broth as a soothing start to your meal or enjoy it as a light, nourishing drink.
6. Any leftover broth can be stored in the refrigerator for future use, ensuring you have a quick, healthy base for soups and stews at your fingertips.

Nutrition Per Serving:

Kcal 20 | Fat: 0g | Carbohydrates: 4g | Protein: 1g | Sodium: 80mg | Potassium: 150mg

This reimagined Country Vegetable Essence celebrates the simplicity and depth of garden-fresh vegetables, simmered gently with a selection of herbs to create a broth that's both nutritious and full of flavor. Perfect for those seeking a light, healthful addition to their diet.

3. Strawberry Bliss Jelly

Skill Level: ★☆☆☆☆

Prep Duration: 5 hrs 10 mins

Cook Duration: 20 mins

Yield: 4 serving

Ingredients:

- ⅓ cup of ripe strawberry pieces, for a burst of fresh flavor
- 1 tbsp. of pure gelatin, the secret to the jelly's perfect texture
- 2 cups of clear, pure water, to create the jelly base
- Organic sweetener equivalent to 3.5 tbsp. of sugar, for natural sweetness

Directions:

1. Begin by boiling the strawberries in one cup of water in a saucepan. Mash the berries as they heat, transforming them into a soft pulp, to extract maximum flavor.
2. Allow the berry mixture to gently simmer for about 8 minutes. This step concentrates the strawberry essence, infusing the water with a deep, fruity taste.
3. While the strawberries are simmering, sprinkle the gelatin over the remaining cup of water in a separate bowl. Let it sit for 5 minutes to "bloom," ensuring it dissolves smoothly later on.
4. Strain the cooked strawberry mixture through a fine sieve, pressing out as much liquid as possible to measure about 2 cups. If necessary, top it up with additional water to reach the desired volume.
5. Return the strained strawberry liquid to the saucepan and reheat gently. Stir in the

sweetener, dissolving it thoroughly for about 1-2 minutes, to sweeten the jelly base.

6. Gradually incorporate the bloomed gelatin into the warm strawberry liquid, stirring until fully dissolved and the mixture is smooth, ensuring no gelatin lumps remain.
7. Pour the jelly mixture into your chosen mold or container. Refrigerate it for 5 hours, or until the jelly sets firm, transforming into a delightful, wobbly treat.
8. Once set, slice the jelly into pieces and enjoy the fresh, fruity flavors of your homemade Strawberry Jelly Delight.

Nutrition Per Serving:

Kcal 55 | Sodium 3 mg | Protein 2 g | Carbs 1 g | Fat 0 g | Potassium: 3 mg

This Strawberry Jelly Delight captures the essence of ripe strawberries in a light, refreshing dessert, ideal for satisfying your sweet tooth with a touch of elegance.

4. Rich Beef Bone Broth

Skill Level: ★★☆☆☆

Prep Duration: 15 mins

Cook Duration: 4 hrs

Yield: 8 serving

Ingredients:

- 1 large carrots, finely diced for a sweet undertone
- 1/3 tsp crushed black pepper, for a mild heat
- 1 bay leaf, for an aromatic depth
- 2 celery ribs, diced to add freshness
- 3 parsley stems, for a herbal accent
- 2 pounds of marrow-filled beef bones, rich in nutrients
- 2 garlic cloves, lightly crushed to unleash their flavor
- Sea salt, adjusted to your taste
- 8 cups of fresh, cold water, to extract the essence
- 2 tbsp apple cider vinegar, to help break down the bones
- 2 sprigs of fresh thyme, for a subtle, earthy aroma

Directions:

1. Place the beef bones in a large pot and submerge them in cold water. This step is crucial for slowly extracting the flavors and nutrients from the bones.
2. Add the diced carrots, celery, garlic, parsley stems, bay leaf, and thyme to the pot. Season the mixture with crushed black pepper and sea salt, then pour in the apple cider vinegar. The vinegar aids in leaching minerals from the bones, enhancing the broth's nutritional value.
3. Bring the water to a boil over medium-high heat. As it begins to boil, foam will form on the surface. Skim off this foam diligently to ensure a clear broth.
4. Once boiling, reduce the heat to a low simmer. Allow the broth to simmer gently for about 4 hours. This slow cooking process is key to extracting a deep flavor and a rich array of nutrients from the bones and vegetables.
5. After simmering, strain the broth through a fine mesh strainer, discarding the solids. This step ensures a smooth, pure elixir full of flavor and nutrition.
6. Let the broth cool slightly before serving. If there's a layer of fat on the surface after cooling, skim it off to enjoy a cleaner taste.
7. Warm up the broth before serving. Any leftovers can be stored in the refrigerator or freezer for future use, serving as a versatile base for soups, stews, or as a nourishing drink on its own.

Nutrition Per Serving:

Kcal 45 | Sodium 60 mg | Protein 8 g | Carbs 1 g | Fat 1 g | Potassium: 100 mg

This revitalized recipe for Savory Meat Bone Elixir simplifies the process of creating a nutrient-rich, flavorful broth that serves as a cornerstone for countless recipes or a comforting, healthful drink.

5. Healing Herbal Broth

Skill Level: ★☆☆☆☆
Prep Duration: 10 mins
Cook Duration: 1 hr
Yield: 4 servings
Ingredients:

- 1 quart of water
- 1/2 cup of fresh parsley, roughly chopped
- 1/4 cup of fresh thyme, roughly chopped
- 1/4 cup of fresh rosemary, roughly chopped
- 2 bay leaves
- 1 teaspoon of whole peppercorns
- 1 tablespoon of lemon juice
- Salt, to taste (optional, based on dietary restrictions and recommendations)

Directions:

1. In a large pot, bring the water to a gentle boil. Add the parsley, thyme, rosemary, bay leaves, and whole peppercorns. These herbs are chosen for their soothing properties and ability to add depth to the broth without needing solid food ingredients.
2. Reduce the heat to low and let the broth simmer uncovered for about 1 hour. This slow cooking process allows the flavors of the herbs to fully infuse the water, creating a rich, aromatic liquid.
3. After simmering, turn off the heat and stir in the lemon juice. The acidity will brighten the broth, adding a layer of complexity to its flavor profile.
4. Use a fine mesh sieve to strain the broth, discarding the solid herbs and peppercorns. This step ensures that the broth is clear and smooth, making it suitable for the liquid phase of the diet.
5. If your dietary plan allows, season the broth with a little salt to enhance its flavors. However, if sodium intake is a concern, the broth is flavorful enough to be enjoyed without additional seasoning.
6. The broth can be served warm or stored in the refrigerator for up to 3 days. Gently reheat as needed, ensuring it's comfortably warm but not too hot to consume.

Nutrition Per Serving:
Kcal < 5 Kcal | Protein 0g | Carbs < 1g (mainly from the herbs, which are not consumed directly) | Fat 0g | Sodium 0mg without added salt (adding salt to taste will increase this value)

This Healing Herbal Broth is designed to offer a comforting and healing beverage option for those in the initial stages of recovery from bariatric surgery, focusing on hydration and ease of digestion.

Advancing to Stage 2: Introducing Full Liquids and Pureed Foods

After the initial phase of clear liquids, the next step in your nutritional journey involves transitioning to a diet that includes full liquids and pureed foods. This stage is crucial for providing your body with the necessary nutrients while still being gentle on your healing digestive system.

Setting Nutritional Objectives for Stage 2

- **Protein Intake**: Strive to consume 80 to 100 grams of protein each day. Between meals, consider protein shakes as a supplementary source to help achieve this goal.
- **Milk and Its Alternatives**: Start with almond milk or soy milk that is sugar-free. During this period, it's advisable to avoid cow's milk due to potential intolerance issues.
- **Gradual Introduction of Supplements**: You can begin to incorporate dietary supplements into your regimen, introducing them one at a time to monitor your body's response.

Exploring Full Liquids and Pureed Food Options

This stage's diet features a consistency thicker than the previous stage, incorporating:

- Low-fat or skim milk, protein-enriched soups, and soy beverages
- Non-dairy and Greek yogurts
- Soft cereals like oatmeal and cream of wheat
- Mashed fruits and creamy soups made from vegetables or legumes
- Fat-free lentils and beans, smoothly pureed
- Cottage cheese mixed with pureed fruits for flavor
- Protein shakes and other nutritional drinks without added sugars
- Smoothies crafted from diluted fruit juices, avoiding added sugars

Guidelines for Successful Stage 2 Diet

While expanding your dietary scope, it's important to:

- Avoid caffeine, carbonated drinks, and sugary foods to prevent complications.
- Introduce new items cautiously, as previous favorites might now cause discomfort.

Tips for Navigating Stage 2 Effectively

- Take your time with meals, aiming for 30-minute sessions to heed your body's fullness signals.
- Consume foods at room temperature or slightly warmed for easier digestion.
- Monitor intake carefully, using measured cups and avoiding straws to prevent swallowing air.
- Enhance protein content in meals and drinks with a bit of protein powder or non-fat powdered milk.
- Keep a detailed food diary for tracking consumption and reactions to specific foods.
- Continue with your multivitamin regimen and any additional supplements recommended by your healthcare provider.

Moving through the second stage of your post-operative diet offers an opportunity to reintroduce a broader range of nutrients into your diet while still respecting your body's current limitations. Follow these guidelines closely, and consult with your healthcare team to tailor your diet to your specific needs, ensuring a smooth transition and continued progress towards recovery and health.

Stage 2 - Recipes

1. Egg-Yogurt Spread

Skill Level: ★☆☆☆☆

Prep Duration: 10 mins

Cook Duration: 0 mins

Yield: 1 serving

Ingredients:

- 1.5 tbsp of light mayonnaise, for a silky texture
- 1 hard-boiled egg, finely mashed for a smooth base
- 1.5 tbsp of low-fat Greek yogurt, adding a tangy creaminess
- A dash of salt and pepper, for seasoning to taste

Directions:

1. Start by combining the mashed hard-boiled egg with the light mayonnaise and low-fat Greek yogurt in a bowl. This mix of ingredients forms the foundation of your creamy spread.
2. Stir the ingredients together until you achieve a uniformly smooth consistency. This step is crucial for ensuring that every bite of the spread has a balanced flavor and creamy texture.
3. Season the mixture with a sprinkle of salt and pepper, adjusting according to your taste preferences. This final touch enhances the natural flavors of the egg and melds the ingredients together.
4. For the best taste experience, refrigerate the spread for a few minutes before serving. This not only cools the spread but also allows the flavors to infuse further.
5. Enjoy your creamy egg spread chilled, perfect as a spread on toast or as a delightful dip for your favorite vegetables.

Nutrition Per Serving:

Kcal 125 | Sodium 190 mg | Protein 8 g | Carbs 2 g | Fat 10 g | Potassium: 60 mg

2. Root Vegetable Harmony Puree

Skill Level: ★★☆☆☆

Prep Duration: 15 mins

Cook Duration: 45 mins

Yield: 4 serving

Ingredients:

- 1 small sweet potato, cubed for sweetness and texture
- 4 cups of water, to soften the vegetables
- 1 leek, finely sliced, for a mild onion flavor
- 1 medium parsnip, diced, adding a woody sweetness
- 1 carrot, chopped into small pieces, for color and taste
- 1 small turnip, cubed, for earthy notes
- ½ onion, minced, to base the puree with depth
- A dash of salt and freshly ground pepper, for seasoning

Directions:

1. Combine the sweet potato, leek, parsnip, carrot, turnip, and onion with water in a large pot. This mix of root vegetables promises a robust base for your puree.
2. Bring the pot to a boil over medium-high heat, then reduce to a simmer. Let the vegetables cook until they're tender and easily pierced with a fork. This slow simmering melds their flavors into a cohesive, comforting blend.
3. Use an immersion blender to puree the mixture right in the pot. Blend until you achieve a creamy, smooth consistency. If the puree is too thick, adjust by adding a bit more water until it reaches your preferred texture.

4. Taste and season with salt and pepper, stirring well to distribute the seasonings evenly. This final step ensures the puree is perfectly flavored to your liking.
5. Serve the puree warm, savoring the rich, velvety combination of sweet and earthy root vegetables. It's a dish that warms the soul and delights the palate.

Nutrition Per Serving:

Kcal 80 | Sodium 20 mg | Protein 1.5 g | Carbs 18 g | Fat 0.2 g | Potassium: 450 mg

3. Garlic Veggie Cream Soup

Skill Level: ★★☆☆☆

Prep Duration: 20 mins

Cook Duration: 40 mins

Yield: 4 serving

Ingredients:

- 3 carrots, thinly sliced
- 1 tsp. olive oil
- 2 leeks, thoroughly cleaned and chopped
- ½ head of cauliflower, broken into florets
- 6 cloves of garlic, finely minced
- ½ head of cabbage, finely shredded
- 1 can (14 oz.) of diced tomatoes
- 4 tsp. tomato paste
- 3½ cups of water
- 4 tbsp. of unsweetened low-fat milk
- Season with salt and pepper to taste

Directions:

1. Start by heating olive oil in a large soup pot over medium heat. Add the leeks, carrots, cauliflower, and cabbage to the pot, sautéing them until they start to soften.
2. Mix in the minced garlic and tomato paste, continuing to cook for a few more minutes until fragrant.
3. Add the diced tomatoes and water to the pot, bringing the mixture to a boil. Once boiling, lower the heat and let it simmer for about 25 minutes, or until the vegetables are tender.
4. Use an immersion blender to puree the soup directly in the pot, blending until smooth. Stir in the milk and heat through for an additional 2 minutes, ensuring the soup reaches a creamy consistency.
5. Season the soup with salt and pepper according to your taste, and serve it hot.

Nutrition Per Serving:

Kcal 120 | Sodium 250 mg | Protein 4 g | Carbs 20 g | Fat 2 g | Potassium: 400 mg

4. Poached Egg Whites

Skill Level: ★☆☆☆☆

Prep Duration: 5 mins

Cook Duration: 12 mins

Yield: 1 serving

Ingredients:

- 2 egg whites, for a light and healthy protein source
- A pinch of salt and pepper, for simple seasoning

Directions:

1. Begin by filling a medium-sized pot with water and bring it to a gentle simmer over medium heat. This initial step ensures the water is hot enough to cook the egg whites without being so vigorous as to break them apart.
2. Crack the egg whites into a small bowl or cup. This allows for a smoother transfer into the water and reduces the risk of the whites dispersing immediately upon contact with the water.
3. Slowly pour the egg whites into the simmering water, doing so carefully to maintain their integrity. The gentle simmer of the water will cook the egg whites evenly, allowing them to firm up without becoming tough.
4. Allow the egg whites to cook undisturbed for about 10-12 minutes. This timing is crucial for achieving the perfect texture—firm yet tender, without any raw parts.
5. Once the egg whites are cooked to your liking, use a slotted spoon to carefully lift them from the water. This method ensures that any excess water drains away, leaving you with perfectly poached egg whites.

6. Season the poached egg whites with a pinch of salt and pepper to enhance their flavor. This final touch adds depth to the delicate taste of the egg whites.
7. Serve the poached egg whites immediately. They are best enjoyed fresh and warm, offering a light, protein-rich component to your meal.

Nutrition Per Serving:

Kcal 34 | Sodium: 110 mg | Protein: 7 g | Carbohydrates: 0 g | Fat: 0 g | Potassium: 54 mg

5. Tropical Blend Smoothie

Skill Level: ★★☆☆☆

Prep Duration: 10 mins

Cook Duration: 0 mins

Yield: 1 serving

Ingredients:

- 1/2 cup non-fat Greek yogurt, for a creamy base that adds a protein punch without the extra calories.
- 1/4 cup frozen mango chunks, to infuse the smoothie with a sweet, tropical flavor and a rich source of vitamins A and C.
- 1/2 cup non-fat milk, to thin the smoothie to the perfect drinking consistency while keeping it light.
- 1/4 cup frozen peach slices, adding a juicy sweetness and contributing to the smoothie's smooth texture.

Directions:

1. In your blender, combine the frozen mango chunks, peach slices, Greek yogurt, and milk. This combination not only adds a refreshing taste but also ensures a balanced mix of nutrients. The Greek yogurt's protein content complements the natural sweetness and vitamins from the fruits, while the milk helps to achieve a perfectly smooth consistency.
2. Blend on high until the mixture becomes creamy and smooth. It's essential to blend thoroughly to ensure there are no fruit chunks left, achieving a silky texture that's easy to enjoy.
3. Serve the smoothie in a tall glass and enjoy immediately to take advantage of its fresh flavor and nutritional benefits.

Nutrition Per Serving:

Kcal 90 | Sodium 50 mg | Protein 7 g | Carbs 13 g | Fat 0 g | Potassium: 150 mg

6. Green Vitality Smoothie

Skill Level: ★★☆☆☆

Prep Duration: 8 mins

Cook Duration: 0 mins

Yield: 1 serving

Ingredients:

- Juice from half a lemon, adding a refreshing zest and vitamin C.
- 2/3 cup of fresh spinach leaves, packed with iron and antioxidants for an energy boost.
- 1/2 tbsp. of powdered almond butter, for a hint of nutty flavor and added protein.
- 1/2 cup of unsweetened coconut milk, providing a creamy base with a tropical touch.
- 1/4 of an avocado, rich in healthy fats and creamy texture.
- 1/2 scoop of unsweetened vanilla protein powder, for muscle repair and sustained energy.

Directions:

1. Begin by adding the coconut milk to your blender, creating a liquid base for the other ingredients to blend smoothly.
2. Incorporate the avocado, spinach, lemon juice, almond butter, and protein powder into the blender. Each ingredient contributes to the smoothie's nutritional profile, offering a blend of vitamins, minerals, and proteins.
3. Blend everything together until the mixture achieves a silky smooth consistency. This step is crucial for ensuring that the spinach and avocado are thoroughly blended, leaving no chunks.

4. Serve the smoothie in a chilled glass to enhance its refreshing taste.

Nutrition Per Serving:

Kcal 150 | Sodium 50 mg | Protein 12 g | Carbs 10 g | Fat 8 g | Potassium: 350 mg

7. Pineapple Coconut Smoothie

Skill Level: ★★☆☆☆

Prep Duration: 12 mins

Cook Duration: 0 mins

Yield: 1 serving

Ingredients:

- 1 tbsp. of desiccated coconut, for a subtle, nutty flavor and added texture.
- 3 tbsp. of non-fat milk, to adjust the smoothie's consistency to your liking.
- 1 cup of frozen pineapple bits, for a sweet, tropical taste and icy texture.
- 1/2 cup of non-fat Greek yogurt, adding creaminess and protein without the fat.

Directions:

1. Place the frozen pineapple bits, Greek yogurt, desiccated coconut, and milk into a high-speed blender. This blend of ingredients promises a tropical flavor profile while ensuring a smooth, creamy consistency that's both nourishing and satisfying.
2. Blend until the mixture is completely smooth. The key is to achieve a velvety texture that makes every sip a delightful experience.
3. Serve the smoothie in a glass immediately to enjoy its frosty goodness. The immediate serving ensures you capture the essence of this tropical treat at its peak freshness and coolness.

Nutrition Per Serving:

Kcal 180 | Sodium 70 mg | Protein 10 g | Carbs 25 g | Fat 4 g | Potassium: 250 mg

8. Peach Tea Infusion

Skill Level: ★☆☆☆☆

Prep Duration: 8 mins

Cook Duration: 4 mins

Yield: 1 serving

Ingredients:

- 1 1/4 cup of protein-enriched water, for a hydrating and muscle-supporting base.
- 1 sachet of peach-flavored tea, offering a fragrant and soothing flavor profile.

Directions:

1. Warm the protein water in a microwave until it reaches a steaming hot temperature. This step not only prepares the water for tea infusion but also activates the protein, making it easier for your body to absorb.
2. Place the peach tea sachet into your favorite mug. The choice of peach tea adds a naturally sweet and aromatic dimension to this warm beverage.
3. Allow the tea to steep according to the directions on the packet. For an extra touch of freshness and flair, garnish your drink with a few fresh mint leaves before enjoying.

Nutrition Per Serving:

Kcal 40 | Sodium 20 mg | Protein 7 g | Carbs 1 g | Fat 0 g | Potassium: 10 mg

9. Chocolate Protein Shake

Skill Level: ★★☆☆☆

Prep Duration: 11 mins

Cook Duration: 0 mins

Yield: 1 serving

Ingredients:

- 1 tbsp. of unsweetened dark cocoa powder, offering a rich, chocolatey depth.
- 1 scoop of chocolate-flavored protein powder, for muscle-building support and added flavor.
- 1 cup of non-fat milk, creating a creamy texture without the extra fat.
- Natural sweetener, adjusted to taste, for a guilt-free sweetness.
- 1 tbsp. of sugar-free chocolate syrup, enhancing the chocolate flavor without the added sugars.

Directions:

1. Start by adding the non-fat milk to your blender, ensuring a smooth base for the other ingredients.
2. Add the dark cocoa powder, protein powder, chocolate syrup, and your choice of sweetener into the blender. This blend not only promises a deliciously rich chocolate taste but also a healthy, protein-packed treat.
3. Blend on high until the mixture is fully combined and reaches a creamy consistency. This step is crucial for dissolving the cocoa and protein powder fully, leaving you with a smooth, satisfying shake.
4. Pour the shake into a tall glass and enjoy immediately, savoring the decadent chocolate flavor and creamy texture.

Nutrition Per Serving:

Kcal 180 | Sodium 200 mg | Protein 22 g | Carbs 10 g | Fat 3 g | Potassium: 450 mg

10. Vanilla Custard

Skill Level: ★★☆☆☆

Prep Duration: 12 mins

Cook Duration: 22 mins

Yield: 1 serving

Ingredients:

- 2 tbsp of sweetener granules, offering a guilt-free sweetness to the custard.
- 1 tsp. of modified starch, to thicken the custard without altering its flavor.
- 3/4 cup of low-fat milk, providing a creamy base with reduced calories.
- 1/4 tsp. of vanilla essence, infusing the custard with its classic, aromatic flavor.
- 1 egg yolks, enriching the custard with a silky texture and a boost of nutrients.

Directions:

1. Begin by whisking together the sweetener, vanilla essence, and milk in a saucepan. Warm the mixture gently over low heat, ensuring it doesn't reach a boil, until the sweetener has fully dissolved.
2. In a separate bowl, vigorously whisk the egg yolks and modified starch together. This mixture will help to thicken the custard, giving it a luxuriously smooth consistency.
3. Gradually incorporate a few tablespoons of the heated milk into the yolk and starch mixture, stirring well to combine. This step tempers the yolks, preventing them from curdling.
4. Slowly add the rest of the milk to the bowl, whisking continuously, then return the entire mixture to the saucepan.
5. Cook over low heat, stirring constantly, until the custard thickens to a creamy consistency. Be patient during this step to avoid any lumps.
6. Once thickened, pour the custard into a serving bowl and enjoy it warm for a comforting treat.

Nutrition Per Serving:

Kcal 120 | Sodium 50 mg | Protein 6 g | Carbs 10 g | Fat 4 g | Potassium: 150 mg

11. Berry Melon Refreshment

Skill Level: ★★☆☆☆

Prep Duration: 11 mins

Cook Duration: 0 mins

Yield: 1 serving

Ingredients:

- 1 scoop of melon nutritional powder, for a refreshing melon flavor and added nutrients.
- 1 cup of low-fat milk, providing a creamy texture and a good source of calcium.
- 2 sprigs of fresh mint, to add a burst of freshness and enhance the drink's aroma.
- 1/2cup of watermelon pieces, offering a juicy sweetness and hydration.
- 2 fresh strawberries, for a tangy sweetness and vibrant color.
- Ice, according to preference, to chill and refresh.

Directions:

1. Place the melon nutritional powder, low-fat milk, fresh mint sprigs, watermelon pieces, strawberries, and ice into a blender. This combination promises a delightful fusion of flavors and textures, balancing the sweetness of berries and melon with the creaminess of milk.

2. Blend all ingredients until the mixture is smooth. The key to a perfect texture is ensuring that the fruits and ice are thoroughly blended, leaving no chunks for a silky-smooth finish.
3. Serve the drink in a glass immediately to enjoy its maximum freshness and flavor. The immediate serving ensures that the mint and melon's aromatic qualities are at their peak.

Nutrition Per Serving:

Kcal 100 | Sodium 60 mg | Protein 6 g | Carbs 15 g | Fat 1.5 g | Potassium: 300 mg

12. Vibrant Veggie Broth

Skill Level: ★★☆☆☆

Prep Duration: 12 mins

Cook Duration: 21 mins

Yield: 2 serving

Ingredients:

- 2 cups of sodium-free chicken stock, serving as a flavorful and healthy base.
- 1/2 cup of skim milk, adding a touch of creaminess without the extra fat.
- 1 cup of thinly sliced zucchini, bringing a mild, sweet flavor and nutrients.
- 1 clove of garlic, minced, to infuse the broth with its aromatic qualities.
- 1 cup of clean water, to dilute and balance the broth.
- Ground black pepper, adjusted to taste, for a spicy note.
- 1/4 tsp. each of onion and garlic seasonings, to enhance the savory depth of the broth.

Directions:

1. Start by combining the sodium-free chicken stock, sliced zucchini, minced garlic, clean water, and seasoning powders (except for the milk) in a large cooking pot. This mix of ingredients is designed to meld together, creating a foundation of flavors that are both robust and comforting.
2. Simmer the mixture over medium heat, allowing the zucchini to become tender, which should take about 17 minutes. The gentle cooking process helps to extract the flavors from the vegetables and seasonings, enriching the stock.
3. Once the zucchini is tender, turn off the heat. Stir in the skim milk to the pot, adding a layer of creamy texture to the broth. Using an immersion blender, carefully blend the mixture until it achieves a creamy consistency. This step integrates the milk smoothly without curdling.
4. Season the finished broth with salt and ground black pepper to your liking. Adjust the seasonings to ensure the broth has a balanced, savory taste.
5. Pour the velvety broth into a bowl, ready to be savored. Serving it warm maximizes the aromatic qualities and comforting warmth of the dish.

Nutrition Per Serving:

Kcal 75 | Sodium 150 mg | Protein 7 g | Carbs 8 g | Fat 1.5 g | Potassium: 300 mg

13. Carrot and Pumpkin Soup

Skill Level: ★★☆☆☆

Prep Duration: 11 mins

Cook Duration: 32 mins

Yield: 2 serving

Ingredients:

- 1/3 tsp. each of turmeric powder and 1/3 tsp. curry spice, to imbue the soup with warmth and a rich palette of flavors.
- A pinch of red pepper flakes, adjusted to your heat preference, for that spicy kick.
- 1 cup of diced carrots, adding sweetness and texture to the blend.
- Seasoning salt & ground pepper, tailored to your taste, to enhance the overall savoriness.

- 1 minced garlic cloves, for a fragrant depth of flavor.
- 1 tsp. of virgin olive oil, providing a subtle, fruity undertone.
- 1/2 cup of light coconut milk, lending a creamy consistency without the heaviness.
- 1 cup of diced pumpkin, for a smooth, velvety base.
- 2 cups low-sodium check stock
- 1/2 tsp. of fresh lemon extract, to introduce a bright, citrusy note.

Directions:

1. Start by sautéing the minced garlic in virgin olive oil in a pot. Quickly stir in the turmeric and curry spices to lightly cook them, releasing their aromatic oils.
2. Add the diced carrots and pumpkin to the pot, giving them a quick toss with the aromatic oil and spices.
3. Pour in the light coconut milk and low-sodium chicken stock, then bring the mixture to a boil. Reduce the heat and simmer until the vegetables are fork-tender.
4. Once the vegetables are soft, use an immersion blender to puree the soup directly in the pot until it reaches a smooth consistency. This step melds all the flavors together seamlessly.
5. Adjust the seasonings with salt and pepper according to your preference, then pour the soup into a bowl to serve while it's still hot.

Nutrition Per Serving:

Kcal 75 | Sodium 150 mg | Protein 2 g | Carbs 15 g | Fat 2 g | Potassium: 400 mg

14. Lemon-Orange Protein Smoothie

Skill Level: ★★☆☆☆

Prep Duration: 11 mins

Cook Duration: 0 mins

Yield: 1 serving

Ingredients:

- Extract from 1/2 lemons, offering a tart and refreshing flavor rich in vitamin C.
- As much purified water as needed, to achieve the desired consistency and hydration.
- Juice from 1 small orange (about 4 oz), for a sweet, citrusy boost full of nutrients.
- 1/2 cup of fresh spinach leaves, adding a dose of iron and antioxidants without altering the fruity taste.
- 4-5 pieces of ice, to chill and thicken the drink.
- 1/2 frozen bananas, to sweeten naturally and add a creamy texture.
- 1 scoop of lemon-flavored nutritional powder, infusing the drink with protein and enhancing the citrus profile.

Directions:

1. Place the lemon extract, orange extract, spinach leaves, ice, frozen banana pieces, and lemon-flavored nutritional powder into a blender. This combination of ingredients ensures a nutrient-packed smoothie with vibrant citrus flavors complemented by the natural sweetness of banana.
2. Blend until the mixture becomes creamy and smooth. The goal here is to fully incorporate all the elements, especially the spinach, so there are no leafy chunks, achieving a pleasingly smooth texture.
3. Serve the smoothie in a chilled glass to maximize refreshment and immediate enjoyment, capturing the essence of the fruits' natural flavors and nutritional benefits.

Nutrition Per Serving:

Kcal 122 | Sodium 12.5 mg | Protein 8.5 g | Carbs 3.5 g | Fat 8.9 g | Potassium: 124 mg

15. Carrot and Ginger Cream Soup

Skill Level: ★★☆☆☆

Prep Duration: 15 mins

Cook Duration: 30 mins

Yield: 2 serving

Ingredients:

- 1 clove of garlic, minced, to add a savory depth.
- 1 tsp. of freshly grated ginger, for its spicy and aromatic flavor.
- 1/4 cup of coconut cream, for a rich, velvety texture.

- 1 cup of vegetable stock, low in sodium, to enhance the soup's base without overpowering it.
- 1/4 tsp. of ground turmeric, for color and its health benefits.
- 1 tsp. of olive oil, to sauté and release the flavors of the aromatics.
- Seasoning salt and freshly ground pepper, to taste, for seasoning.
- 1 cup of carrots, diced, to provide sweetness and body to the soup.

Directions:

1. Heat olive oil in a pot over medium heat. Once hot, add the diced carrots and sauté until they start to soften, introducing a sweet base to the soup.
2. Stir in the minced garlic and grated ginger, cooking for a few minutes until fragrant, to layer the soup's flavor profile.
3. Sprinkle in the turmeric and season with salt and pepper, mixing well to distribute the spices evenly.
4. Pour in the coconut cream and vegetable stock, and bring to a gentle boil to combine all the flavors.
5. Reduce the heat and let the soup simmer for about 25 minutes, allowing the ingredients to meld together fully.
6. Use a hand blender to puree the soup until creamy, ensuring a smooth and consistent texture.
7. Taste and adjust the seasoning as necessary, then serve the soup warm, embracing its comforting and aromatic qualities.

Nutrition Per Serving:

Kcal 90 | Sodium 60 mg | Protein 2 g | Carbs 15 g | Fat 4 g | Potassium: 315 mg

16. Lemon Berry Energy Smoothie

Skill Level: ★☆☆☆☆

Prep Duration: 12 mins

Cook Duration: 0 mins

Yield: 1 serving

Ingredients:

- ½ cup (about 2.5 oz.) of blueberries, rich in antioxidants and offering a burst of berry flavor.
- The juice from 1/4 of a lemon, adding a refreshing citrus twist.
- 1/2 cup of water, to help blend the ingredients smoothly.
- 1/4 of a frozen banana, to provide natural sweetness and a creamy texture.
- Natural sweetener, like stevia, adjusted to taste for a hint of sweetness without added sugar.
- 1 heaped tsp. of lemon-flavored vitamin supplement, for an extra nutritional boost.
- 1/2 cup of fresh spinach, introducing iron and additional nutrients without overpowering the fruity flavors.

Directions:

1. Add the blueberries, lemon juice, water, frozen banana, natural sweetener, lemon-flavored vitamin supplement, and fresh spinach into a powerful blender. This blend of ingredients ensures a mix of refreshing citrus, sweet berry flavors, and essential nutrients.
2. Blend at high speed until the mixture becomes smooth and creamy. Ensuring a consistent texture is key to a delightful smoothie experience.
3. Pour the smoothie into a glass and enjoy it immediately to make the most of its vibrant flavors and energy-boosting properties.

Nutrition Per Serving:

Kcal 90 | Sodium 15 mg | Protein 2 g | Carbs 20 g | Fat 0.5 g | Potassium: 200 mg

17. Strawberry Yogurt Treat

Skill Level: ★☆☆☆☆

Prep Duration: 12 mins

Cook Duration: 0 mins

Yield: 1 serving

Ingredients:

- Zero-calorie sweetener to taste, for a guilt-free sweetness.
- 4 ripe strawberries, adding a juicy and fresh berry flavor.
- 2 tbsp. of light whipped cream, for a fluffy, light texture.
- 1/2 cup of non-fat Greek yogurt, providing a creamy base rich in protein.

Directions:

1. Begin by mashing the strawberries gently in a mixing bowl, releasing their natural juices and flavors.
2. Stir in the Greek yogurt, blending it with the mashed strawberries and sweetener until smooth. This step combines the creamy texture of yogurt with the sweetness of strawberries and the desired amount of sweetener.
3. Carefully fold the whipped cream into the mixture, ensuring it stays light and airy.
4. Refrigerate the mixture until chilled, enhancing its flavors and providing a refreshing cold dessert.

Nutrition Per Serving:

Kcal 60 | Sodium 30 mg | Protein 6 g | Carbs 8 g | Fat 1 g | Potassium: 150 mg

18. Easy Tomato and Basil Soup

Skill Level: ★★☆☆☆

Prep Duration: 15 mins

Cook Duration: 25 mins

Yield: 2 serving

Ingredients:

- 1/4 of an onion, finely diced, to add a subtle sweetness and depth of flavor.
- 4 fresh tomatoes, diced, for a rich and tangy base.
- 1 cloves of garlic, minced, infusing the soup with aromatic depth.
- Salt & freshly ground pepper, adjusted to taste, for seasoning.
- 1/2 tsp. of olive oil, for sautéing the vegetables and adding a hint of richness.
- 1 tbsp. of fresh basil leaves, finely chopped, to bring a fresh and herby brightness.
- 1 cup of water or vegetable stock, added as needed, to achieve the desired consistency.

Directions:

1. Heat the olive oil in a saucepan over medium heat. Sauté the diced onion and minced garlic until they become translucent, laying the foundational flavors for the soup.
2. Add the diced tomatoes and chopped basil to the pot, stirring well. Allow the mixture to simmer until the tomatoes soften, blending the flavors beautifully.
3. Season the simmering mixture with salt and freshly ground pepper to enhance the natural flavors of the ingredients.

4. Use an immersion blender to purée the soup until it reaches a smooth and creamy consistency. Add water or vegetable stock to adjust the thickness as desired.
5. Continue to simmer the soup for an additional 5 minutes to meld the flavors further. Serve the soup hot for a comforting and nutritious meal.

Nutrition Per Serving:

Kcal 80 | Sodium 150 mg | Protein 2 g | Carbs 12 g | Fat 2 g | Potassium: 400 mg

19. Mexican-Style Egg with Beans

Skill Level: ★★☆☆☆

Prep Duration: 15 mins

Cook Duration: 20 mins

Yield: 1 serving

Ingredients:

- 1 tbsp. of non-fat Greek yogurt, adding a creamy texture without the extra calories.
- 2 tbsp. of canned black beans, drained and rinsed, to introduce a fiber-rich component.
- 2 tbsp. of diced turkey sausage, providing lean protein with a hint of smokiness.
- 1/8 tsp. of ground cumin, offering a warm, earthy flavor typical of Mexican cuisine.
- 1 tbsp. of chopped cilantro, for a fresh, herbal note.
- 1 medium egg, a versatile protein source.
- Smoked paprika to taste, for a subtle, smoky heat.

Directions:

1. In a bowl, whisk together the egg, cumin, smoked paprika, and Greek yogurt. This mixture will form the flavorful base of your dish.
2. Heat a skillet over medium heat and brown the diced turkey sausage, adding a savory depth to the meal.
3. Pour the egg mixture over the browned sausage in the skillet, cooking until the eggs begin to set.
4. Gently fold in the black beans and chopped cilantro, mixing them in for a brief moment to warm through.
5. Transfer the skillet's contents into a blender, add a little water for consistency, and blend until smooth.
6. Serve the dish warm, garnished with an extra sprinkle of cilantro for a fresh touch.

Nutrition Per Serving:

Kcal 120 | Sodium 300 mg | Protein 12 g | Carbs 5 g | Fat 5 g | Potassium: 150 mg

20. Herb-Infused Chicken Minced with Bean Puree

Skill Level: ★★☆☆☆

Prep Duration: 15 mins

Cook Duration: 20 mins

Yield: 1 serving

Ingredients:

- 1/4 cup of minced chicken, providing a lean protein base.
- 2 tbsp. of fresh parsley, finely chopped, to add a burst of flavor and color.
- 1 tbsp. of fresh cilantro, finely chopped, for its distinctive, aromatic touch.
- 1/4 tsp. of apple cider vinegar, to brighten the dish with a hint of acidity.
- 1/8 tsp. of ground oregano, for its earthy, slightly bitter undertone.
- 1/8 tsp. of paprika, to introduce a smoky sweetness.
- 1 small garlic clove, minced, to lay a foundation of pungent, spicy flavor.

Directions:

1. Warm a skillet over medium heat with a small amount of water. This method starts the cooking process without adding extra fat.
2. Season the minced chicken with paprika and oregano before adding it to the skillet. Cook until fully browned, adding a bit more water as necessary to prevent sticking.
3. In a separate bowl, prepare the herb puree by blending the parsley, cilantro, apple cider vinegar, and garlic until smooth.

4. Once the chicken is cooked, combine it with the herb puree in the skillet, ensuring the chicken is evenly coated and the flavors meld together.
5. Transfer this mixture to a serving plate, garnishing with additional cilantro or parsley if desired, and serve warm.

Nutrition Per Serving:

Kcal 80 | Sodium 100 mg | Protein 12 g | Carbs 1 g | Fat 2 g | Potassium: 150 mg

21. Seasoned Turkey and Bean Fusion

Skill Level: ★★☆☆☆

Prep Duration: 15 mins

Cook Duration: 25 mins

Yield: 1 serving

Ingredients:

For the Bean Component:

- 1/4 cup pinto beans, rinsed and drained, to introduce a hearty texture and rich fiber.
- 1 tbsp. fresh cilantro, finely chopped, offering a burst of fresh flavor.
- 1/4 cup low-sodium chicken broth, providing a savory liquid base.
- 1/4 tsp. minced garlic, adding a subtle, aromatic depth.

For the Turkey:

- 1/4 cup ground turkey, a lean source of protein.
- A pinch (1/8 tsp.) each of chili powder, cumin, garlic powder, and paprika, creating a robust and warming spice blend.

Directions:

1. Begin by heating a splash of water in a pan over medium heat. Sauté the minced garlic until just fragrant.
2. Pour in the chicken broth and add the pinto beans. Bring to a boil, then lower the heat and simmer until the beans are tender.
3. Stir the fresh cilantro into the bean mixture, then remove from heat and set aside.
4. In a separate pan, toast the spice mixture briefly before adding the ground turkey. Cook until the turkey is thoroughly browned.
5. In a food processor, combine the cooked bean mixture and the turkey. Process until you achieve a smooth, well-blended consistency.
6. Serve the blend warm, perhaps garnished with extra cilantro for a fresh touch.

Nutrition Per Serving:

Kcal 110 | Sodium 70 mg | Protein 11 g | Carbs 8 g | Fat 2 g | Potassium: 250 mg

22. Chicken and Bean Mole Fusion

Skill Level: ★★☆☆☆

Prep Duration: 20 mins

Cook Duration: 25 mins

Yield: 1 serving

Ingredients:

Bean Mixture:

- 1/4 cup black beans, rinsed
- 1 tsp. fresh cilantro, finely chopped
- 1/4 cup chicken broth
- 1/4 tsp. minced garlic

Turkey Mixture:

- 1/4 cup ground turkey
- A pinch (1/8 tsp.) each of chili powder, cumin, garlic powder, and paprika

Almond Mixture:

- 1 tbsp ground almonds
- 1 tsp cocoa powder (unsweetened)
- 1 tbsp fresh cilantro, finely chopped
- 1/4 cup low-sodium chicken broth

Directions:

1. Start by sautéing minced garlic with a bit of water in a pot.
2. Introduce the chicken and season with paprika, cumin, and other spices, cooking until fully browned.
3. In a blender, mix almonds, cilantro, cocoa powder, and a bit of chicken broth until achieving a smooth texture.
4. Combine this almond mixture with the black beans in the pot containing the chicken, stirring well.
5. Allow the combined mixture to simmer, letting the flavors blend together thoroughly.

6. Serve the fusion hot, possibly garnished with additional cilantro for enhanced flavor.

Nutrition Per Serving:

Kcal 120 | Sodium 70 mg | Protein 12 g | Carbs 10 g | Fat 4 g | Potassium: 250 mg

23. Holiday Protein Eggnog

Skill Level: ★★☆☆☆

Prep Duration: 10 mins

Cook Duration: 0 mins

Yield: 1 serving

Ingredients:

- 1/8 tsp. each of ground cinnamon and 1/8 nutmeg for that classic eggnog spice.
- 1 cup of crushed ice to chill and thicken the beverage.
- 1 servings of vanilla-flavored protein shake for a nutritious, protein-packed base.
- 1/4 tsp. of rum flavoring to mimic the traditional eggnog taste without the alcohol.

Directions:

1. Add the ground cinnamon, nutmeg, crushed ice, vanilla-flavored protein shake, and rum flavoring into a blender. This combination ensures a festive blend of flavors and textures.
2. Blend the ingredients on high until the mixture becomes smooth and frothy, creating a creamy consistency reminiscent of classic eggnog.
3. Immediately pour the eggnog into a glass and enjoy the festive, protein-rich drink.

Nutrition Per Serving:

Kcal 160 | Sodium 250 mg | Protein 30 g | Carbs 5 g | Fat 2.5 g | Potassium: 300 mg

24. Pumpkin Spice Protein Smoothie

Skill Level: ★★☆☆☆

Prep Duration: 12 mins

Cook Duration: 0 mins

Yield: 1 serving

Ingredients:

- 1/8 tsp. each of ground cinnamon and 1/8 nutmeg to evoke the essence of pumpkin spice.
- 1/4 cup of pumpkin puree, offering a rich, autumnal flavor and fiber.
- 1 scoop of vanilla protein powder, for muscle repair and recovery.
- 1 cup of crushed ice, to chill and thicken the smoothie.
- 1/2 cups of skimmed milk, providing a low-fat, creamy base.
- 1/2 tsp. of Stevia or a similar sweetener, to taste, for a hint of sweetness without the added sugar.

Directions:

1. Combine the pumpkin spice, pumpkin puree, vanilla protein powder, crushed ice, skimmed milk, and sweetener in a blender. This mix ensures a harmonious blend of fall flavors with a protein boost.
2. Blend the ingredients on high until the mixture achieves a smooth, frothy consistency, perfect for a refreshing smoothie.
3. Pour the smoothie into a glass and enjoy it immediately, capturing the essence of fall in a nutritious, protein-packed drink.

Nutrition Per Serving:

Kcal 180 | Sodium 150 mg | Protein 25 g | Carbs 15 g | Fat 1 g | Potassium: 300 mg

25. Creamy Butternut Squash and Ginger Soup

Skill Level: ★★☆☆☆

Prep Duration: 30 mins

Cook Duration: 0 mins

Yield: 1 serving

Ingredients:

- Butternut squash, peeled and diced: 3/4 cup, to provide a sweet, nutty base rich in vitamins.
- Fresh ginger, grated: 1/4 tsp, adding a zesty flavor and digestive benefits.
- Cinnamon powder: 1/8 tsp, for a hint of warming spice.
- Nutmeg, ground: A pinch, to complement the butternut squash with its sweet and nutty aroma.

- Unsweetened almond milk: 1/2 cup, for a creamy texture without the heaviness of dairy.
- Protein powder, vanilla: 1/2 scoop, to support muscle recovery and add a smooth, sweet note.
- Monk fruit sweetener: 1/2 tsp, offering a calorie-free sweetness.
- Water: 1/4 cup, to adjust the soup's consistency to your liking.

Directions:

1. Begin by simmering the diced butternut squash in water until it's tender and easily mashable. This softens the squash, making it perfect for blending into a smooth soup.
2. Once the butternut squash is cooked, blend it together with the grated fresh ginger, cinnamon, nutmeg, almond milk, protein powder, and monk fruit sweetener. This combination ensures a blend of flavors that are both comforting and invigorating.
3. Adjust the soup's consistency by adding water as needed, aiming for a creamy yet pourable texture. This step allows you to tailor the soup to your personal preference, ensuring it's neither too thick nor too thin.
4. Gently reheat the blended soup, stirring constantly to prevent sticking or uneven heating. This ensures your soup is warm and inviting, perfect for nourishing the body and soul.
5. Serve this creamy butternut squash and ginger soup warm, garnishing with a sprinkle of cinnamon or nutmeg if desired. This final touch not only adds to the visual appeal but also enhances the soup's aromatic qualities.

Nutrition Per Serving:

Kcal 125 | Sodium 120 mg | Protein 15 g | Carbs 15 g | Fat 2 g | Potassium 400 mg

26. Lemon-Garlic Salmon Puree

Skill Level: ★☆☆☆☆

Prep Duration: 7 mins

Cook Duration: 0 mins

Yield: 1 serving

Ingredients:

- 2 oz of boneless salmon, ensuring a rich source of omega-3 fatty acids.
- 1/8 tsp of garlic granules to add a savory depth.
- 1/2 tbsp of low-fat mayonnaise, offering creaminess without excessive calories.
- A squeeze of fresh lemon (1/4 tsp), providing a zesty, fresh lift to the puree.

Directions:

1. Start by carefully draining the can of salmon to remove any excess liquid.
2. Place the salmon in a food processor, adding the garlic granules, low-fat mayonnaise, and a fresh squeeze of lemon for a bright burst of flavor.
3. Process the mixture until it achieves a smooth consistency, ideal for a spread or dip. For the best flavor, enjoy this puree chilled, allowing the flavors to meld beautifully.

Nutrition Per Serving:

Kcal 90 | Sodium 120 mg | Protein 10 g | Carbs 1 g | Fat 5 g | Potassium 180 mg

27. Baked Ricotta Herb Casserole

Skill Level: ★☆☆☆☆

Prep Duration: 8 mins

Cook Duration: 18 mins

Yield: 1 serving

Ingredients:

- 3 oz of creamy ricotta cheese, providing a base that's both rich and light.
- 1 tbsp of semi-skimmed cheese, for added depth and a touch of creaminess.
- 1/2 tsp of freshly snipped oregano, bringing a bright, aromatic note.
- 1/8 tsp of onion powder, for subtle savory undertones.

- Seasoning to taste, allowing for a personalized flavor profile.

Directions:

1. Begin by preheating your oven to 355°F, setting the stage for a warm, evenly cooked dish.
2. Lightly grease a baking dish suited for a single serving to ensure nothing sticks during the baking process.
3. In a mixing bowl, combine the ricotta cheese, semi-skimmed cheese, fresh oregano, onion powder, and your choice of seasoning. Stir these ingredients until well blended, ensuring the flavors are thoroughly mixed.
4. Transfer the cheese mixture into your prepared baking dish. Place it in the oven, allowing it to bake until it turns golden brown on top, signaling it's perfectly cooked through and ready to enjoy.

Nutrition Per Serving:

Kcal 120 | Sodium 150 mg | Protein 10 g | Carbs 3 g | Fat 7 g | Potassium 90 mg

28. Creamy Yogurt & Garlic Shrimp

Skill Level: ★★☆☆☆

Prep Duration: 6 mins

Cook Duration: 8 mins

Yield: 1 serving

Ingredients:

- 5 deveined shrimps, chosen for their succulent taste and texture.
- 1 tbsp of non-fat Greek yogurt, adding a creamy tang without the added fat.
- 1 minced garlic clove, for a rich, aromatic flavor.
- 1 tbsp of snipped chives, providing a mild onion-like essence.

Directions:

1. Begin by lightly sautéing the shrimps in a pan with just a bit of water, cooking until they've turned a lovely shade of pink, indicating they're just done.
2. Add the minced garlic to the pan, stirring it in with the shrimps, and cook for an additional minute to allow the garlic to soften and its flavor to infuse the shrimps.
3. Take the pan off the heat, and gently fold in the non-fat Greek yogurt and snipped chives into the shrimps, combining until the shrimps are evenly coated in this creamy, herb-infused mixture.
4. Serve this blend as a deliciously creamy and flavorful dish, perfect for a nutritious and satisfying meal.

Nutrition Per Serving:

Kcal 80 | Sodium 130 mg | Protein 14 g | Carbs 2 g | Fat 1 g | Potassium 120 mg

29. Chocolate Almond Butter Protein Smoothie

Skill Level: ★☆☆☆☆

Prep Duration: 6 mins

Cook Duration: 0 mins

Yield: 1 serving

Ingredients:

- 1 scoop of dark cocoa protein powder, offering a rich, chocolaty flavor along with a protein boost.
- 1/2 cup of almond milk, providing a nutty, creamy base.
- 1/2 cup of ice, to add chill and texture.
- 1 tablespoon of creamy almond butter, for smoothness and a hint of savory nuttiness.

Directions:

1. Begin by adding the dark cocoa protein powder, almond milk, ice, and creamy almond butter into your blender. This combination promises a decadent yet healthy treat.
2. Process the mixture on high until it achieves a silky smooth consistency, ensuring that every sip is perfectly blended.
3. Pour the smoothie into your favorite glass, ready to be enjoyed as a deliciously indulgent yet nutritious drink.

Nutrition Per Serving:

Kcal 180 | Sodium 150 mg | Protein 20 g | Carbs 10 g | Fat 7 g | Potassium 200 mg

30. Herb Pinto Bean Mash

Skill Level: ★★☆☆☆

Prep Duration: 10 mins

Cook Duration: 10 mins

Yield: 1 serving

Ingredients:

- 1 tablespoon of fresh cilantro, finely chopped for a burst of freshness.
- 1/3 cup of pinto beans, thoroughly washed and drained, serving as the hearty base of the dish.
- A blend of 1/8 teaspoon each of garlic, chili, cumin, and onion powder, creating a complex flavor profile.
- 1/4 cup of vegetable stock, adding depth and moisture to the beans.

Directions:

1. Warm a skillet over medium heat and add the pinto beans along with a splash of the vegetable stock, simmering the mixture for about 2 minutes to infuse the flavors.
2. Sprinkle in the mixed seasonings, pouring in the remainder of the vegetable stock, then bring the mixture to a boil. Continue cooking until the liquid has significantly reduced, concentrating the flavors.
3. Use a potato masher to gently mash the beans to your desired consistency, creating a rich and textured bean mash.
4. Finish by stirring in the fresh cilantro, which will add a bright, herbaceous note to the dish. Serve this bean mash warm, enjoying the robust flavors and comforting texture.

Nutrition Per Serving:

Kcal 70 | Sodium 150 mg | Protein 5 g | Carbs 12 g | Fat 0.5 g | Potassium 180 mg

Stage 3: Transitioning to a Semi-Solid/Soft Foods Diet

Foods to Include:

- **Lean Meats**: This includes ground beef and any other low-fat meats, ensuring your protein intake remains high.
- **Seafood and Fish**: All varieties are encouraged, offering essential omega-3 fatty acids.
- **Eggs**: A versatile protein source that can be prepared in various soft-cooked methods.
- **Cottage Cheese and Greek Yogurt**: High in protein and calcium, these dairy options are beneficial for muscle and bone health.
- **Beans**: A great plant-based protein source.
- **Protein Bars**: Opt for bars low in sugar and high in protein.
- **Non-starchy Vegetables**: These provide vital nutrients without excessive carbohydrates.
- **Fruits**: Aim for soft fruits that are easy to digest.

Foods to Avoid:

- **Tough Meats**: Steak and other hard-to-chew meats are not suitable at this stage.
- **Certain Vegetables**: Peas, potatoes, and corn are to be avoided due to their starchy content.
- **Starches**: Bread, pasta, rice, oatmeal, and cereal are too complex for the recovering digestive system.
- **Fried Foods**: These can be hard to digest and high in unhealthy fats.
- **Sugary Foods**: Refined sugars and desserts can disrupt your nutritional balance.
- **Nuts and Nut Butters**: These should be limited due to their fat content and potential difficulty in digestion.

Nutritional Guidelines and Meal Ideas:

Seven to eight weeks post-surgery, your diet should start incorporating more texture with semi-solid and soft foods, focusing on nutrition and ease of digestion.

- **Protein-Rich Foods**: Slow-cooked meats, canned tuna, crab, or chicken are excellent for ensuring adequate protein intake.
- **Mashed Alternatives**: Consider refried beans, mashed chickpeas, tofu, or lentils for variety.
- **Dairy**: Low-fat, creamy cheeses can add flavor and nutrients to your meals.
- **Softly Prepared Meals**: Opt for tender stews, chilis, and flaky fish such as trout or salmon.
- **Vegetables and Fruits**: Choose well-cooked or soft vegetables and tender fruits to ensure you're getting necessary vitamins without strain on your digestive system.

Maintaining hydration is crucial, but remember the 30/30 rule to avoid drinking 30 minutes before and after meals to optimize digestion and nutrient absorption.

Eating Techniques and Habits:

- Your meals should primarily consist of proteins, with minimal inclusion of carbohydrates and fats.
- Pay attention to food labels to understand the nutritional content of your meals.

- Example meals might include scrambled or soft-boiled eggs, tofu, stewed chicken, well-cooked vegetables, baked fish, and sugar-free, low-fat yogurt.
- It's important to eat slowly, taking small bites and thoroughly chewing your food to achieve a near-liquid consistency, mimicking the action of a blender.
- Avoid consuming beverages during meals to prevent filling up on liquids instead of nutrient-rich foods.

This stage is about gradually reintroducing your system to a broader range of foods while ensuring that your diet remains balanced and supportive of your recovery and weight loss goals. Always consult with a healthcare provider or dietitian to tailor your diet plan to your specific needs and progress.

Stage 3 – Recipes

1. Chickpea & Crispy Bacon Deviled Eggs

Skill Level: ★★☆☆☆

Prep Duration: 20 mins

Cook Duration: 0 hrs

Yield: 14 servings (1 half egg each)

Ingredients:

- 7 hard-boiled eggs, a perfect base for a creamy filling.
- 2 tbsp. canned chickpeas, rinsed and drained for a hint of nuttiness.
- 1 tbsp. fresh dill, finely chopped, to add a fresh, herby flavor.
- 3 tbsp. Greek yogurt, creating a creamy, tangy texture.
- 2 slices of crispy bacon, crumbled, for a savory crunch.
- 1 tsp. Dijon mustard, adding a mild spicy kick.
- A pinch of paprika for a colorful garnish.

Directions:

1. Begin by slicing the hard-boiled eggs in half lengthwise, a simple step that prepares them for the delightful filling.
2. Carefully remove the yolks, placing them in a mixing bowl, setting the stage for a rich and creamy base.
3. To the yolks, add the chickpeas, chopped dill, Greek yogurt, and Dijon mustard. This combination of ingredients is mixed until smooth, creating a flavorful and creamy texture.
4. Next, the yolk mixture is spooned or piped back into the egg whites, filling them with the creamy, flavorful mixture.
5. Finally, each egg half is garnished with crumbled bacon and a sprinkle of paprika, adding a savory crunch and a dash of color.
6. Chill before serving to allow the flavors to meld together, creating a refreshing and satisfying appetizer.

Nutrition Per Serving (1 half):

Kcal 55 | Sodium 120 mg | Protein 5 g | Carbs 1.5 g | Fat 3 g | Potassium 100 mg

This recipe transforms traditional deviled eggs into a gourmet treat with the unique addition of chickpeas and crispy bacon, offering a delicious way to enjoy a protein-packed snack.

2. Baked Ricotta with Spinach and Sun-dried Tomatoes

Skill Level: ★★☆☆☆

Prep Duration: 15 mins

Cook Duration: 25 mins

Yield: 4 servings

Ingredients:

- 1/2 cup of part-skim ricotta cheese, offering a creamy texture with less fat.
- 1/4 cup of low-fat mozzarella cheese, shredded for melty goodness.

- 2 tbsp. of finely chopped sun-dried tomatoes, bringing a tangy sweetness.
- 1/2 cup of fresh spinach, chopped for a healthy, verdant touch.
- 1 tbsp. of grated Parmesan cheese for a sharp, savory finish.

Directions:

1. Begin by preheating your oven to 355°F (180°C), ensuring it's ready for baking. Lightly grease 4 individual ramekins to prevent sticking.
2. Heat a non-stick pan over medium heat and wilt the spinach until it softens, which will integrate beautifully with the cheeses.
3. In a mixing bowl, combine the softened spinach, sun-dried tomatoes, ricotta, mozzarella, and Parmesan cheeses. This creates a rich, flavorful mixture that's both comforting and nutritious.
4. Evenly distribute the cheese and spinach mixture among the prepared ramekins, creating individual servings that are perfect for portion control.
5. Bake in the preheated oven for about 18 to 22 minutes, or until the mixture is bubbly and golden on top, offering a visually appealing and deliciously aromatic dish.

Nutrition Per Serving:

Kcal 110 | Sodium 250 mg | Protein 10 g | Carbs 4 g | Fat 6 g | Potassium 200 mg

3. Lemon-Spinach Soup

Skill Level: ★★☆☆☆

Prep Duration: 15 mins

Cook Duration: 25 mins

Yield: 4 servings

Ingredients:

- 1 tbsp. of olive oil for sautéing, adding a hint of richness.
- 3.5 cups of low-sodium vegetable broth, forming the soup's flavorful base.
- Juice of 1 lemon, infusing the soup with a vibrant citrus note.
- 1 medium white onion, chopped, for a subtle sweetness and depth.
- 1/2 lb. of potatoes, diced, contributing a comforting thickness.
- 1 lb. of frozen spinach, thawed and drained, for a green, nutritious punch.
- 2 garlic cloves, minced, to add a robust aroma and taste.
- Salt & pepper to taste, for seasoning.

Directions:

1. In a large pot, heat the olive oil over medium heat. Sauté the minced garlic and chopped onion until they become translucent, laying the foundation for the soup's flavors.
2. Add the diced potatoes and low-sodium vegetable broth to the pot. Bring to a boil, then reduce the heat to a simmer. Cook until the potatoes are tender, blending the flavors together.
3. Stir in the thawed and drained spinach, and continue to cook for an additional 5 minutes, letting the spinach fully integrate into the soup.
4. Using a blender, purée the soup until smooth. Season with salt, pepper, and lemon juice to taste, balancing the zestiness with the soup's richness.
5. Serve the soup warm, inviting a comforting and nourishing experience with each spoonful.

Nutrition Per Serving:

85 Kcal | 250 mg Sodium | 4 g Protein | 12 g Carbs | 1.5 g Fat | 500 mg Potassium

4. Scrambled Eggs with Protein-Rich Black Bean Sauce

Skill Level: ★★☆☆☆

Prep Duration: 20 mins

Cook Duration: 25 mins

Yield: 4 servings

Ingredients: For the Eggs:

- 4 eggs, whisked together for fluffiness.
- Salt & pepper to taste, for simple seasoning.

For the Black Bean Sauce:

- 1.5 tbsp. unflavored whey protein powder, adding a protein boost.

- 1/2 cup green enchilada sauce, for a tangy flavor kick.
- 1 cup rinsed canned black beans, for fiber and protein.
- 1/4 cup chicken broth, to thin and enrich the sauce.

Directions:

1. Warm the black beans in a skillet over medium heat, starting the base of your sauce.
2. Stir in the enchilada sauce and let it cook for 3 minutes, allowing the flavors to meld. Add the chicken broth and continue to cook until well combined.
3. Use a blender to purée the bean mixture until smooth. Let it cool slightly, then stir in the whey protein powder until fully incorporated.
4. In another pan, scramble the eggs seasoned with salt and pepper until they reach your desired consistency.
5. Serve the fluffy scrambled eggs topped with the smooth, protein-rich black bean sauce for a nourishing start to your day.

Nutrition Per Serving:

110 Kcal | 250 mg Sodium | 10 g Protein | 8 g Carbs | 4 g Fat | 400 mg Potassium

5. Savory Pork & Bean Soup with a Yogurt Twist

Skill Level: ★★☆☆☆

Prep Duration: 15 mins

Cook Duration: 30 mins

Yield: 8 servings

Ingredients:

- 1 tsp. each of paprika, onion powder, and garlic powder, for a flavorful base.
- 2/3 cup each of pinto beans and black beans, rinsed and drained, adding heartiness and texture.
- 1/3 tsp. dried oregano, for a hint of herbal note.
- 1 tsp. cumin, for a warm, earthy spice.
- 0.6 lb. lean ground pork, providing rich protein.
- 1/3 cup chopped cilantro, for a fresh garnish.
- 4 cups low-sodium chicken broth, creating a light but flavorful soup base.
- 1 ½ cups chopped zucchini, adding freshness and a crisp texture.
- 1 ½ tsp. olive oil, for sautéing.
- 1/3 cup low-fat Greek yogurt, for a creamy, tangy topping.

Directions:

1. In a large pot, toast the paprika, onion powder, and garlic powder for a few minutes to release their aromas.
2. Add olive oil and sauté the ground pork until it's fully browned, ensuring a rich flavor.
3. Mix in the chicken broth, both types of beans, and zucchini. Bring the mixture to a simmer and cook until the zucchini is tender, blending the flavors harmoniously.
4. Use a blender to partially purée the soup, leaving some texture for interest. Serve the soup hot, garnished with a dollop of Greek yogurt and a sprinkle of fresh cilantro.

Nutrition Per Serving:

105 Kcal | 150 mg Sodium | 10.5 g Protein | 9 g Carbs | 3.5 g Fat | 470 mg Potassium

6. Blueberry Bliss Yogurt Bowl

Skill Level: ★★☆☆☆

Prep Duration: 10 mins

Cook Duration: 0 mins

Yield: 1 serving

Ingredients:

- 1 packets of sweetener (such as Stevia), for a guilt-free sweetness.
- 5 oz. of low-fat Greek yogurt, creamy and rich in protein.
- 2 tbsp. of blueberries (previously frozen), for a burst of juicy flavor.

Directions:

1. Warm the blueberries in the microwave for 20 seconds to release their natural juices and sweetness.
2. In a bowl, blend the Greek yogurt smoothly and incorporate the sweetener to taste.

3. Carefully fold the warmed blueberries into the yogurt, allowing streaks of juice to swirl through.

Nutrition Per Serving:

85 Kcal | 55 mg Sodium | 9 g Protein | 8 g Carbs | 0.5 g Fat | 140 mg Potassium

7. Banana-Spinach Energy Smoothie

Skill Level: ★★☆☆☆

Prep Duration: 10 mins

Cook Duration: 0 mins

Yield: 1 serving

Ingredients:

- 1/3 cup low-fat Greek yogurt, for a creamy base high in protein.
- 1/2 scoop vanilla-flavored protein powder, for a boost of protein and flavor.
- 1/4 ripe banana, for natural sweetness and energy.
- 1/2 cup fresh spinach leaves, packed with nutrients for vitality.
- 1/2 tbsp. nut butter (almond preferred), for healthy fats and added richness.
- 1/2 cup water, to achieve the perfect smoothie consistency.

Directions:

1. Combine the Greek yogurt, vanilla protein powder, banana, fresh spinach leaves, nut butter, and water in a blender.
2. Blend on high until the mixture is completely smooth. Adjust water if necessary to reach your desired thickness.
3. Pour the smoothie into a glass and enjoy immediately for a refreshing and energizing treat.

Nutrition Per Serving:

150 Kcal | 70 mg Sodium | 12 g Protein | 15 g Carbs | 5g Fat | 300 mg Potassium

8. Creamy Orange Delight Smoothie

Skill Level: ★★☆☆☆

Prep Duration: 10 mins

Cook Duration: 0 mins

Yield: 1 serving

Ingredients:

- 2 oz. non-fat yogurt, for a light and smooth base.
- 1/2 scoop vanilla-flavored protein powder, for a sweet protein kick.
- 1/2 packet sweetener, to enhance the smoothie's sweetness.
- 2 oz. water, to thin the smoothie to your liking.
- 1/4 cup mandarin orange slices, for a citrus burst.
- 1 ice cube made from non-fat milk, to chill and thicken.

Directions:

1. Place the non-fat yogurt, vanilla protein powder, sweetener, water, mandarin orange slices, and the milk ice cube into a blender.
2. Blend all ingredients until you achieve a smooth, creamy texture.
3. Serve the smoothie chilled for a refreshing and nutritious drink.

Nutrition Per Serving:

90 Kcal | 45 mg Sodium | 9 g Protein | 10 g Carbs | 0.5 g Fat | 150 mg Potassium

9. Savory Vegetable & Egg Tart

Skill Level: ★★☆☆☆

Prep Duration: 15 mins

Cook Duration: 35 mins

Yield: 4 serving

Ingredients:

- 1 cup of 1% milk, for a light, creamy base.
- ½ cup each of sautéed zucchini & bell pepper, offering a sweet and slightly crunchy texture.
- ½ cup grated mozzarella cheese, for gooey, melty goodness.
- 4 large eggs, whisked to bind all the ingredients together.
- 1 tbsp. olive oil, to enrich the flavor and ensure a moist, tender finish.

Directions:

1. Begin by preheating your oven to 365°F (185°C), setting the stage for a gentle, even bake.
2. In a large bowl, combine the whisked eggs, milk, olive oil, and mozzarella cheese. Stir until the mixture is homogenous.
3. Fold in the sautéed zucchini and bell pepper, distributing them evenly throughout the mixture.
4. Grease a baking dish with a bit of olive oil or butter to prevent sticking. Pour the egg and vegetable mixture into the dish.
5. Bake in the preheated oven for 30 to 35 minutes, or until the tart is set and the top is lightly golden.
6. Once done, slice into wedges and serve warm, offering a delicious, nourishing meal that's perfect for any time of day.

Nutrition Per Serving:

Kcal 180 | Sodium 200 mg | Protein 12 g | Carbs 6 g | Fat 10 g | Potassium 180 mg

10. Citrus Bliss Smoothie

Skill Level: ★★☆☆☆

Prep Duration: 10 mins

Cook Duration: 0 mins

Yield: 1 serving

Ingredients:

- 2 oz. non-fat yogurt, for a light, creamy texture.
- 1/2 scoop vanilla-flavored protein powder, for a protein boost and sweet vanilla essence.
- 1/2 packet sweetener, to taste.
- 2 oz. water, to adjust consistency.
- 1/4 cup mandarin orange slices, for a tangy citrus burst.
- 1 ice cube made from non-fat milk, for a chilled, smooth blend.

Directions:

1. Add non-fat yogurt, vanilla protein powder, sweetener, water, mandarin orange slices, and the non-fat milk ice cube into a blender.
2. Blend until the mixture reaches a creamy consistency. Ensure everything is well combined and smooth.
3. Serve the smoothie chilled for a refreshing and energizing drink.

Nutrition Per Serving:

90 Kcal | 45 mg Sodium | 10 g Protein | 10 g Carbs | 0.5 g Fat | 150 mg Potassium

11. Berry Fusion Smoothie Bowl

Skill Level: ★☆☆☆☆

Prep Duration: 10 mins

Cook Duration: 0 mins

Yield: 2 servings

Ingredients:

- 1 scoop of protein powder, for a muscle-friendly boost.
- ½ cup of diet grape-cranberry blend, offering a tart and refreshing twist.
- ½ cup of low-fat milk, providing a smooth, creamy base.
- ½ cup of mixed frozen berries, bursting with antioxidants and sweet flavors.

Directions:

1. Place the protein powder, diet grape-cranberry blend, low-fat milk, and mixed frozen berries into a blender.
2. Blend until the mixture reaches a creamy, smooth consistency. This ensures every spoonful is infused with the delightful flavors and nutrients of the berries.
3. Serve the smoothie bowl immediately, reveling in its creamy texture and berry-packed goodness.

Nutrition Per Serving:

110 Kcal | 70 mg Sodium | 10 g Protein | 10 g Carbs | 2 g Fat | 150 mg Potassium

12. Velvety Avocado & Berry Smoothie

Skill Level: ★☆☆☆☆

Prep Duration: 10 mins

Cook Duration: 0 mins

Yield: 2 servings

Ingredients:

- ¼ cup of blueberries, rich in antioxidants and bursting with flavor.
- 1 tsp of organic sweetener, adding just the right touch of sweetness.
- ¼ of a ripe avocado, providing creamy texture and healthy fats.
- 1 cup of strawberries, for a juicy, tangy kick.
- ½ cup of low-fat Greek yogurt, adding protein and creamy consistency.
- ½ cup of reduced-fat milk, to blend everything into a smooth delight.

Directions:

1. Add the blueberries, organic sweetener, ripe avocado, strawberries, low-fat Greek yogurt, and reduced-fat milk into a blender.
2. Blend until the mixture becomes velvety smooth, ensuring a luxurious texture that's both indulgent and healthy.
3. Serve the smoothie immediately, enjoying the rich, creamy blend of berry flavors and the nutritional benefits of avocado.

Nutrition Per Serving:

180 Kcal | 55 mg Sodium | 10 g Protein | 20 g Carbs | 7 g Fat | 250 mg Potassium

13. Hearty Mediterranean Bean Soup

Skill Level: ★★☆☆☆

Prep Duration: 20 mins

Cook Duration: 1 hr

Yield: 4 servings

Ingredients:

- 1 medium zucchini, diced, for a fresh, mild flavor.
- 1 stalk of celery, chopped, adding a crisp texture.
- 1 tbsp of extra-virgin olive oil, for sautéing and richness.
- 2 medium carrots, chopped, for sweetness and color.
- 4 cups of vegetable broth, as a flavorful soup base.
- 1 ½ cups of fresh spinach, chopped, for nutrients and greenery.
- 1 can of roasted tomatoes (15 oz.), to add depth and tang.
- ½ medium white onion, diced, for foundational flavor.
- 1 can of Cannellini beans (15 oz.), for protein and body.
- 2 garlic cloves, finely chopped, for aromatic warmth.
- 1 tbsp of tomato concentrate, for intensified tomato flavor.

Seasonings:

- Salt, black pepper, and chili flakes, adjusted to preference, for seasoning.
- ¾ tbsp each of dried rosemary, sage, and parsley, for Mediterranean aromatics.

Directions:

1. Heat the olive oil in a large pot over medium heat. Sauté the carrots, celery, and onions for 4 minutes, until they start to soften.
2. Add the zucchini and garlic; continue cooking for another 3 minutes, letting the flavors meld.

3. Stir in the roasted tomatoes, Cannellini beans, tomato concentrate, and the seasonings. Pour in the vegetable broth and bring to a simmer. Cook on low heat for 50 minutes, allowing the soup to thicken slightly and flavors to deepen.
4. Mix in the fresh spinach and continue to simmer for another 10 minutes, until the spinach is wilted and fully integrated into the soup.
5. If a smoother consistency is desired, lightly blend some of the soup with a blender, then reintegrate. Serve the soup warm, adjusting seasonings as necessary.

Nutrition Per Serving:

140 Kcal | 400 mg Sodium | 6 g Protein | 22 g Carbs | 4 g Fat | 550 mg Potassium

14. Cherry-Chocolate Smoothie Delight

Skill Level: ★☆☆☆☆

Prep Duration: 10 mins

Cook Duration: 0 mins

Yield: 2 servings

Ingredients:

- 1 cup of cold water, as the smoothie's refreshing base.
- 1 scoop of cocoa drink mix, for a deep chocolate flavor.
- 2 tbsp of tart cherry concentrate, adding a bright, tangy contrast.

Directions:

1. Combine the cold water, cocoa drink mix, and tart cherry concentrate in a mixing bowl. Stir well until all ingredients are thoroughly mixed.
2. Place the mixture in the refrigerator to chill for a few minutes. This enhances the flavors and cools the drink to perfection.
3. Serve the smoothie delight chilled, enjoying the rich chocolate taste with the zesty cherry twist.

Nutrition Per Serving:

90 Kcal | 70 mg Sodium | 10 g Protein | 12 g Carbs | 1 g Fat | 150 mg Potassium

15. Kale-Infused Turkey Bites

Skill Level: ★★☆☆☆

Prep Duration: 20 mins

Cook Duration: 40 mins

Yield: 4 servings

Ingredients:

- 1 ½ cups of fresh kale, finely chopped, to infuse a nutrient-rich green touch.
- 1 tsp of apple vinegar, for a subtle tangy accent.
- 1 tsp of garlic essence, to enhance flavor depth.
- 1 tbsp of grated parmesan, for a savory, cheesy hint.
- 1 lb of lean turkey mince, providing a protein-packed base.
- 1 organic egg, to bind the ingredients together.
- 2 tbsp each of chopped cilantro & mint, adding fresh, aromatic notes.
- ¼ cup of low-fat Greek yogurt, for a creamy, tangy sauce.

Directions:

1. Begin by preheating your oven to 350°F (175°C) and lightly grease a baking tray to prevent sticking.
2. In a large bowl, combine the turkey mince, finely chopped kale, organic egg, and grated parmesan. Mix until well combined.
3. Shape the mixture into 16 evenly sized portions, forming bite-sized balls or patties according to preference.
4. Place on the greased tray and bake in the preheated oven for 30 minutes, turning them halfway through to ensure even cooking.
5. While the turkey bites cook, whisk the low-fat Greek yogurt with a bit of warm water, apple vinegar, chopped cilantro, and mint to create a smooth, flavorful sauce.
6. Once cooked, remove the turkey bites from the oven, let them cool slightly, and then drizzle the yogurt sauce over them before serving.

Nutrition Per Serving:

140 Kcal | 80 mg Sodium | 22 g Protein | 3 g Carbs | 5 g Fat | 280 mg Potassium

16. Spicy Chicken Cheese Bites

Skill Level: ★★☆☆☆

Prep Duration: 20 mins

Cook Duration: 25 mins

Yield: 4 servings

Ingredients:

- ½ lb of chicken mince, a lean base for these savory bites.
- 2 tbsp of soft low-fat cream cheese, adding creamy texture without the guilt.
- ¼ cup of shredded mozzarella and ¼ cup of cheddar, for a delightful cheese pull and flavor.
- 2 tbsp of spicy wing sauce, to bring heat and zest to every bite.

Directions:

1. Start by preheating your oven to 350°F (175°C) to ensure it's ready for baking.
2. In a mixing bowl, combine the chicken mince, soft low-fat cream cheese, shredded mozzarella, shredded cheddar, and spicy wing sauce. Mix until all ingredients are evenly distributed.
3. Shape the mixture into small, bite-sized balls. This size ensures a quick cook time and easy snacking.
4. Arrange the chicken cheese balls on a greased baking dish and cover with aluminum foil to keep them moist while cooking.
5. Bake in the preheated oven for 20-25 minutes or until fully cooked through. The covering helps prevent them from drying out.
6. Let the chicken cheese balls cool slightly before serving, allowing the flavors to set and the cheese to be just the right texture.

Nutrition Per Serving (2 Balls):

120 Kcal | 300 mg Sodium | 14 g Protein | 1 g Carbs | 7 g Fat | 250 mg Potassium

17. Ricotta-Laced Scrambled Eggs

Skill Level: ★★☆☆☆

Prep Duration: 15 mins

Cook Duration: 10 mins

Yield: 1 serving

Ingredients:

- 1/4 cup of softened ricotta, adding a creamy texture and rich taste.
- 2 large eggs, whisked, for a fluffy and protein-rich base.
- 1 tbsp. of fresh parsley, chopped, for a fresh garnish.
- Seasoning blend to taste, for personalized flavor enhancement.
- 2 tbsp of almond milk, to make the eggs tender and light.

Directions:

1. In a bowl, whisk together the eggs, almond milk, and your choice of seasoning blend until well combined.
2. Heat a non-stick skillet over medium heat. Pour in the egg mixture, stirring gently.
3. As the eggs begin to set, gently fold in the ricotta cheese, incorporating it into the eggs for a creamy, delicious texture.
4. Continue cooking to your desired consistency. Just before finishing, sprinkle with the chopped parsley for a burst of freshness and color.
5. Serve the scrambled eggs warm, enjoying the rich, comforting blend of flavors and textures.

Nutrition Per Serving:

190 Kcal | 220 mg Sodium | 17 g Protein | 3 g Carbs | 12 g Fat | 180 mg Potassium

18. Velvety Zucchini & Potato Soup

Skill Level: ★★☆☆☆

Prep Duration: 20 mins

Cook Duration: 40 mins

Yield: 4 servings

Ingredients:

- 4 cups of vegetable broth, providing a savory liquid base.
- ½ white onion, diced, for a foundational aromatic layer.
- ¼ tsp. ground celery, adding depth with its subtle, earthy notes.
- 1/3 cup of low-fat yogurt, for a creamy consistency and tang.
- 1 clove of garlic, minced, for a hint of sharpness.
- 1 tbsp. of olive oil, for sautéing and adding richness.
- ¼ tsp. dried basil, introducing a sweet, herbal undertone.
- A pinch of crushed red pepper, for a slight kick of heat.
- ¼ tsp. ground white pepper, for a piquant spice note.
- ¼ tsp. dried oregano, adding earthy, minty layers.
- 1/2 cup of low-fat grated mozzarella cheese, for melty, cheesy goodness.
- 2 small golden potatoes, cubed, for heartiness and texture.
- ¼ tsp. sea salt, to enhance overall flavors.
- 3 cups diced zucchini, the star vegetable, bringing freshness and body.
- 1 tbsp. Worcestershire sauce, for umami depth and complexity.

Directions:

1. Heat the olive oil in a large saucepan over medium heat. Add the diced onion and sauté until translucent, then mix in the minced garlic and cook for another minute, setting the flavor base.
2. Stir in the ground celery, dried basil, oregano, white pepper, and a pinch of crushed red pepper, followed by the zucchini. Sauté everything together for a few minutes to meld the flavors.
3. Add the Worcestershire sauce, vegetable broth, and cubed potatoes to the pot. Bring the mixture to a boil, then lower the heat and let it simmer for about 30 minutes, or until the vegetables are tender.
4. Use an immersion blender or a standard blender to purée the soup until it achieves a smooth, creamy texture. Be careful if using a standard blender by blending in batches and allowing steam to escape.
5. Serve the soup hot, topped with a sprinkle of low-fat grated mozzarella cheese for a final touch of creamy indulgence.

Nutrition Per Serving:

150 Kcal | 360 mg Sodium | 7 g Protein | 18 g Carbs | 6 g Fat | 520 mg Potassium

19. Savory Slow-Cooked Chicken Curry

Skill Level: ★★☆☆☆

Prep Duration: 15 mins

Cook Duration: 4 hrs 15 mins

Yield: 4 servings

Ingredients:

- Seasoning mix: ¼ tsp., to rub the chicken and infuse it with flavor.
- Garam masala: 2 tbsp., for the rich, warm spices characteristic of curry.
- ½ red onion, thinly sliced, to add sweetness and depth.
- 1 lb. of boneless, skinless chicken breast, the protein base of the dish.
- ½ green bell pepper, julienned, for a crunchy, mild flavor.
- ½ cup frozen green beans, for added texture and color.
- 2 medium radishes, diced, for a peppery bite.
- 1 cup vegetable broth, to create a flavorful cooking liquid.
- 1 tsp. minced ginger, for its sharp, aromatic quality.

- 1 cup light coconut cream, for a creamy, tropical richness.
- 2 cups broccoli rice, as a nutritious, low-carb base.
- 1 tbsp. rice flour mixed with 1 tbsp. filtered water, to thicken the curry sauce.

Directions:

1. Start by rubbing the chicken breast with the seasoning mix, coating it evenly for flavor.
2. Place the seasoned chicken in a slow cooker, along with the coconut cream, vegetable broth, red onion, green bell pepper, green beans, and radishes.
3. Set the slow cooker to low and let it cook for 4 hours, allowing the ingredients to meld together and the chicken to become tender.
4. Mix the rice flour with filtered water to create a slurry. Stir this into the slow cooker, blending it thoroughly with the other ingredients.
5. Continue to cook for an additional 15 minutes, letting the curry thicken slightly.
6. Serve the chicken curry warm over a bed of broccoli rice, offering a comforting and nutritious meal.

Nutrition Per Serving:

220 Kcal | 300 mg Sodium | 26 g Protein | 10 g Carbs | 9 g Fat | 500 mg Potassium

20. Almond-Crusted Fish with Tomato Basil Topping

Skill Level: ★★☆☆☆

Prep Duration: 12 mins

Cook Duration: 35 mins

Yield: 2 servings

Ingredients:

- ¼ cup of crushed almonds, for a crunchy, nutty crust.
- 1 tsp. of extra virgin olive oil, to enhance flavor and aid in cooking.
- 1 tsp. of fresh basil, chopped, for a fragrant, herby lift.
- 2 (each about 4 oz) of tender white fish fillet, the star of the dish.
- 1 tsp. of lime juice, for a citrusy tang that complements the fish.
- 1/3 cup of chopped tomatoes, adding freshness and a slight acidity.

Directions:

1. Preheat the oven to 380°F (193°C), setting the stage for a perfect bake.
2. Mix lime juice and olive oil in a baking tray. This mixture will help to flavor and moisten the fish.
3. Lay the fish fillets in the tray, making sure each is well-coated with the lime and oil mixture. Bake for about 20 minutes, until the fish is nearly cooked through.
4. In the meantime, pulse the crushed almonds, fresh basil, and chopped tomatoes in a blender to achieve a coarse, textured paste. This blend forms the heart of the nutty tomato topping.
5. After the fish has baked for 20 minutes, evenly spread the almond-tomato mixture over the fillets. Return to the oven and bake for an additional 5 minutes, allowing the topping to slightly crisp up and marry its flavors with the fish.
6. Serve the fish warm, enjoying the harmonious blend of nutty, tangy, and herby flavors that elevate the tender, flaky texture of the fish.

Nutrition Per Serving:

160 Kcal | 100 mg Sodium | 20 g Protein | 3 g Carbs | 8 g Fat | 300 mg Potassium

21. Cranberry & Herb-Infused Turkey Meatballs

Skill Level: ★★☆☆☆

Prep Duration: 12 mins

Cook Duration: 25 mins

Yield: 4 servings

Ingredients:

- 1/4 cup of oats, acting as a binder and adding texture.
- 2 tbsp of unsweetened dried cranberries, for a sweet and tart contrast.
- 1 egg, to help bind the mixture together.
- 1 lb of lean turkey mince, providing a healthy protein base.

- 1/8 tsp. of white pepper, for a subtle, sharp flavor.
- 1/4 cup of grated emmental, adding a mild, nutty cheese flavor.
- A pinch of pink salt, for seasoning.
- 1/4 tsp. of dried tarragon, introducing a slight bittersweet, aromatic taste.

Directions:

1. Begin by preheating your oven to 355°F (180°C) and lightly grease a baking sheet to prevent sticking.
2. In a large bowl, thoroughly combine the oats, dried cranberries, eggs, lean turkey mince, white pepper, grated emmental, pink salt, and dried tarragon. Mix until all ingredients are evenly distributed.
3. Shape the mixture into 1.7 oz. balls, creating uniform-sized meatballs for even cooking.
4. Place the meatballs on the prepared baking sheet and bake in the preheated oven for about 22 minutes, or until they are golden brown and cooked throughout.
5. Serve the meatballs warm, enjoying the unique combination of savory turkey, sweet cranberries, and aromatic herbs.

Nutrition Per Serving:

140 Kcal | 150 mg Sodium | 18 g Protein | 6 g Carbs | 5 g Fat | 270 mg Potassium

22. Berry Protein Jello Cups

Skill Level: ★★☆☆☆

Prep Duration: 30 mins

Cook Duration: 1 hr 30 mins (including chilling time)

Yield: 4 servings

Ingredients:

- ½ cups of assorted berries, for a fresh and colorful topping.
- 1 package (0.3 oz) of unsweetened raspberry jello mix, creating a vibrant, jiggly base.
- 4 oz. of low-fat, low-sugar custard, for a creamy layer of sweetness.
- 1 scoop of vanilla protein powder, to boost the protein content and enhance flavor.

Directions:

1. Begin by dissolving the raspberry jello mix in one cup of hot water in a large bowl. Allow it to cool for a few minutes to avoid degrading the protein powder.
2. Once the jello mix is slightly cooled, whisk in the vanilla protein powder until the mixture is smooth and homogeneous.
3. Evenly distribute the jello and protein mixture among four glasses, creating a base layer in each. Place the glasses in the refrigerator to set, ensuring they are level for an even jello formation.
4. After the jello has set, which should take about an hour or so, top each glass with an ounce of the low-fat, low-sugar custard, adding a smooth, creamy texture contrast to the firm jello.
5. Garnish each cup with a generous helping of assorted fresh berries, adding a burst of flavor and a pop of color on top.

Nutrition Per Serving:

60 Kcal | 55 mg Sodium | 7 g Protein | 7 g Carbs | 1 g Fat | 75 mg Potassium

23. Savory Spinach & Feta Herb Pie

Skill Level: ★★☆☆☆

Prep Duration: 15 mins

Cook Duration: 40 mins

Yield: 4 servings

Ingredients:

- ½ white onion, chopped, for a base of sweetness and depth.
- 3.5 oz. of reduced-fat feta cheese, for tangy, creamy bites.
- ¼ cup of skim milk, adding moisture without excess fat.
- 10 oz. of thawed chopped spinach, rich in vitamins and minerals.
- 1 tbsp. of vegetable oil, for sautéing and greasing the pan.
- ¼ cup of fresh parsley, chopped, for a burst of freshness.
- A hint of red chili flakes, to introduce a gentle heat.

- Salt & black pepper, to taste, for seasoning.
- 2 large eggs, beaten, to bind the pie filling together.
- ¼ cup of whole wheat flour, for a healthier, hearty texture.

Directions:

1. Preheat your oven to 350°F (175°C) and prepare a 9-inch baking pan with a light coating of vegetable oil to prevent sticking.
2. Heat the oil in a skillet over medium heat and sauté the chopped onion until it becomes translucent, setting the foundation for the pie's flavor.
3. Stir in the spinach, parsley, red chili flakes, salt, and pepper. Cook for an additional 2 minutes, allowing the flavors to meld and the spinach to slightly wilt.
4. In a separate bowl, whisk together the skim milk, beaten eggs, and whole wheat flour until the mixture is smooth and consistent.
5. Combine the spinach mixture with the egg and flour mixture, ensuring everything is evenly distributed.
6. Transfer this blend into the prepared baking dish, spreading it out evenly. Crumble the reduced-fat feta cheese over the top, adding a creamy layer of flavor.
7. Bake in the preheated oven for approximately 30 minutes, or until the pie is set and the top is lightly golden.

Nutrition Per Serving:

140 Kcal | 320 mg Sodium | 8 g Protein | 10 g Carbs | 7 g Fat | 200 mg Potassium

24. Seafood Spice Crab Salad

Skill Level: ★☆☆☆☆

Prep Duration: 10 mins

Cook Duration: 0 mins

Yield: 2 servings

Ingredients:

- 8 oz. of imitation crab chunks, for a seafood flavor without the splurge.
- 1 scoop of plain protein powder, to boost the protein content.
- 2 tbsp. of reduced-fat mayonnaise, for creaminess with fewer calories.
- A sprinkle of seafood spice, to enhance the maritime flavor.

Directions:

1. Begin by tearing the imitation crab into smaller, bite-sized pieces in a large bowl, making the base of your salad.
2. Add the plain protein powder to the crab, mixing thoroughly to coat the pieces evenly. This step ensures that the protein is well-integrated into the dish.
3. Stir in the reduced-fat mayonnaise, blending it with the crab and protein powder until the mixture achieves a creamy consistency.
4. Finish with a sprinkle of seafood spice, adjusting the amount to suit your taste preferences, and give the salad a final stir to distribute the flavors evenly.
5. Chill the mixture in the refrigerator for about 30 minutes before serving. This resting period allows the flavors to meld together and the salad to cool, enhancing its refreshing quality.

Nutrition Per Serving:

150 Kcal | 350 mg Sodium | 15 g Protein | 8 g Carbs | 6 g Fat | 120 mg Potassium

25. Robust Veggie & Bean Chili

Skill Level: ★★☆☆☆

Prep Duration: 25 mins

Cook Duration: 35 mins

Yield: 4 servings

Ingredients:

- ½ large yellow onion, diced, for a savory sweetness.
- ½ green and ½ yellow bell pepper, chopped, adding color and crunch.
- 3 cups of filtered water, for the chili base.
- 11 oz. of assorted beans (black, red, and pinto), drained, for texture and protein.
- 1 tsp. of lime zest, for a citrusy zing.
- 2 garlic cloves, minced, for a flavorful aroma.

- 1 tbsp. of extra virgin olive oil, for sautéing the veggies.
- ½ medium zucchini, diced, for a mild, garden-fresh addition.
- 8 oz of fresh tofu, cubed, as a hearty protein source.
- 14.5 oz. of low-sodium diced tomatoes, for richness and moisture.
- 1 tbsp. of organic chili seasoning, for that classic chili flavor.
- Sea salt & ground black pepper, to taste, for seasoning.

Directions:

1. Heat the olive oil in a large pot over medium heat. Begin by sautéing the garlic, onion, both bell peppers, and zucchini until they start to soften, laying down a flavorful foundation.
2. Add the assorted beans, diced tomatoes, chili seasoning, and water to the pot. Stir to combine all the ingredients.
3. Bring the mixture to a boil, then lower the heat to simmer. Allow it to cook for about 20 minutes, letting the flavors meld together.
4. Stir in the tofu cubes and lime zest. Season with sea salt and ground black pepper. Continue to simmer for an additional 10 minutes, allowing the tofu to absorb the flavors.
5. For a thicker consistency, lightly mash some of the beans and veggies with a potato masher right in the pot, then serve warm.

Nutrition Per Serving:

180 Kcal | 160 mg Sodium | 14 g Protein | 24 g Carbs | 3 g Fat | 400 mg Potassium

26. High-Protein Chicken Salad

Skill Level: ★☆☆☆☆

Prep Duration: 20 mins

Cook Duration: 0 mins

Yield: 2 servings

Ingredients:

- 1 tbsp. of mayonnaise and honey mustard each, for creaminess and a hint of sweetness.
- ½ cup of boiled edamame, adding a pop of color and plant-based protein.
- ¼ tsp. each of Herbs de Provence and onion powder, for a fragrant seasoning blend.
- ¼ cup of Greek yogurt, offering a tangy base and boosting the protein content.
- Salt & white pepper, to taste, for perfect seasoning.
- Half a green onion, sliced, for a fresh, sharp accent.
- 6 oz. of roasted chicken breast, shredded, providing a hearty, protein-packed main ingredient.

Directions:

1. In a large mixing bowl, combine the mayonnaise, honey mustard, boiled edamame, Herbs de Provence, onion powder, Greek yogurt, salt, white pepper, green onion, and shredded roasted chicken breast.
2. Stir the mixture until all ingredients are thoroughly combined, ensuring each bite is flavorful and well-seasoned.
3. Taste the salad and adjust the seasoning as needed to suit your palate.
4. For the best flavor integration, refrigerate the salad for about an hour before serving. This chilling time allows the flavors to meld together beautifully.

Nutrition Per Serving:

220 Kcal | 340 mg Sodium | 22 g Protein | 10 g Carbs | 10 g Fat | 350 mg Potassium

27. Creamy Parmesan Cauliflower & Bean Purée

Skill Level: ★★☆☆☆

Prep Duration: 30 mins

Cook Duration: 1 hr 30 mins

Yield: 4 servings

Ingredients:

- 10 oz. white Cannellini beans, washed, for a creamy texture and added protein.
- 1 cup fresh water, to help in cooking the vegetables.
- A pinch of salt, for seasoning.

- 1 cup reduced-sodium chicken stock, for flavor and liquid.
- ¼ tsp. ground white pepper, for a subtle spice.
- 2 garlic bulbs, to infuse the dish with aromatic depth.
- 3 cups fresh cauliflower pieces, for a nutritious and light base.
- ¼ cup grated Parmesan, for a rich, umami flavor.

Directions:

1. Start by preheating your oven to 350°F (177°C) to get it ready for the roasting step.
2. In a saucepan, bring the water, chicken stock, and garlic to a boil. Add the cauliflower pieces once boiling.
3. Cover and let it simmer for 5 to 7 minutes, just until the cauliflower begins to soften.
4. Carefully remove the garlic and about half of the cooking liquid. Stir in the Parmesan cheese and Cannellini beans to the remaining mixture.
5. Use a handheld blender to purée the mixture until smooth and creamy. Transfer this creamy purée into an oven-proof dish.
6. Bake in the preheated oven for 20-25 minutes, allowing the flavors to meld and the top to achieve a slight golden crust.
7. Serve warm, offering a comforting and nutritious side or main dish.

Nutrition Per Serving:

130 Kcal | 200 mg Sodium | 9 g Protein | 16 g Carbohydrates | 4 g Fat | 300 mg Potassium

28. Savory Turkey Taco Casserole

Skill Level: ★★☆☆☆

Prep Duration: 30 mins

Cook Duration: 1 hr 30 mins

Yield: 4 servings

Ingredients:

- 1 fresh zucchini, diced, adding a crisp, green texture.
- 1 organic sweet onion, diced, for a foundation of sweetness.
- ½ sachet of taco mix, to infuse the dish with traditional taco flavors.
- 1 lb. of ground turkey meat, providing a lean protein base.
- 8 oz. of canned tomatoes & chilies, for a spicy, tangy kick.
- 4 oz. of fat-free refried beans, for a creamy, satisfying layer.
- 1 cup of Mexican-style cheese blend, for gooey, melted deliciousness.
- 1 clove of garlic, minced, adding aromatic depth.
- 10 oz. of washed black beans, for added texture and protein.

Directions:

1. Begin by preheating your oven to 350°F (177°C) to get it ready for baking.
2. Lightly spray a pan with oil and sauté the minced garlic along with the diced zucchini and sweet onion. Once tender, transfer them to a separate container.
3. In the same pan, brown the ground turkey meat, then mix it into the container with the veggies.
4. Stir the taco mix, canned tomatoes & chilies into the turkey and vegetable mixture, ensuring everything is well combined.
5. Spread this flavorful mixture evenly in a 13x9-inch casserole dish.
6. Layer the fat-free refried beans over the mixture, then sprinkle the entire top with the Mexican-style cheese blend.
7. Bake in the preheated oven for about 30 minutes, until the cheese is bubbly and golden.
8. Allow the casserole to cool slightly before serving, ensuring it's the perfect temperature to enjoy.

Nutrition Per Serving:

250 Kcal | 480 mg Sodium | 24 g Protein | 18 g Carbohydrates | 10 g Fat | 400 mg Potassium

29. BBQ-Flavored Turkey Muffin Loaves

Skill Level: ★★☆☆☆

Prep Duration: 30 mins

Cook Duration: 1 hr 10 mins (40 mins bake time + cooling)

Yield: 4 servings

Ingredients:

- 2 tbsp. of savory Worcestershire sauce, for a deep, umami base.
- ¼ cup of low-carb bread crumbs, to help bind the loaves without adding too many carbs.
- ½ cup of chopped onion, for sweetness and texture.
- 1 lb. of lean ground turkey breast, providing a high-protein, low-fat foundation.
- Salt & pepper to season, enhancing the natural flavors of the turkey.
- 1 fresh egg, to act as a binding agent for all the ingredients.
- ¼ cup of sugar-free BBQ sauce, for smoky, tangy notes throughout the loaves.

Toppings:

- An additional ¼ cup of sugar-free BBQ sauce, to glaze and add a final BBQ flavor boost.

Directions:

1. Preheat your oven to 350°F (177°C). Lightly grease 9 muffin slots to ensure easy removal after baking.
2. In a large mixing bowl, thoroughly combine the Worcestershire sauce, low-carb bread crumbs, chopped onion, ground turkey breast, salt, pepper, egg, and 0.5 cup of sugar-free BBQ sauce. Mix until all ingredients are evenly distributed.
3. Evenly fill the prepared muffin slots with the turkey mixture. This will create individual mini loaves, perfect for portion control.
4. Glaze the top of each mini loaf with the additional sugar-free BBQ sauce, adding a rich, glossy finish.
5. Bake in the preheated oven for approximately 40 minutes, or until the loaves are cooked through and the tops are caramelized.
6. Allow the mini loaves to cool for a bit before serving, making them easier to handle and enhancing their flavor.

Nutrition Per Serving:

130 Kcal | 360 mg Sodium | 18 g Protein |

5 g Carbohydrates | 3 g Fat | 240 mg Potassium

30. Smokey Andouille and Bean Stew

Skill Level: ★★☆☆☆

Prep Duration: 30 mins

Cook Duration: 8 hrs

Yield: 4 servings

Ingredients:

- ½ fresh sweet onion, chopped, adding a subtle sweetness.
- ½ lb. of dry Northern beans, providing a hearty base with plenty of fiber.
- 1 fresh tomatoes, seedless and diced, for natural acidity and freshness.
- ½ tsp Kosher salt, to enhance the flavors.
- 4 oz. of diced Andouille sausage, for a spicy, smoky protein.
- 2 cloves of fresh garlic, minced, to infuse the dish with aromatic depth.
- ½ fresh jalapeno, seedless and diced, introducing a gentle heat.
- 1 tsp. of Cajun seasoning, for that classic Southern spice.
- 2 cups of chicken stock, creating a rich and savory broth.
- ½ tsp. of smoked paprika spice, adding a layer of smokiness.
- 1 cup of fresh water, ensuring the stew has the perfect consistency.

Directions:

1. Begin by browning the diced Andouille sausage in a pre-heated, oil-sprayed pan. This step is crucial for developing a deep, smoky flavor.
2. Add the chopped tomatoes and onions to the pan, cooking just long enough for them to begin to soften and meld their flavors with the sausage.

3. Stir in the minced garlic, cooking for about a minute to prevent it from burning while releasing its flavor.
4. Transfer the sausage mixture to a slow cooker, then add the dry Northern beans, fresh jalapeno, Cajun seasoning, smoked paprika spice, chicken stock, and fresh water. Stir well to combine all the ingredients evenly.
5. Set your slow cooker to a low setting and let the stew cook for approximately 8 hours. This slow cooking process allows the flavors to deepen and the beans to become perfectly tender.
6. For those who prefer a thicker texture, give the stew a brief blend before serving, but ensure to leave plenty of texture.
7. Serve the stew warm, enjoying the complex layers of flavor that have developed over the hours.

Nutrition Per Serving:

220 Kcal | 270 mg Sodium | 18 g Protein |
22 g Carbohydrates | 6 g Fat | 250 mg Potassium

Stage 4: Transitioning to a Regular Diet

Around four to six weeks after your surgery, you'll transition into what's known as the General Phase. This stage is crucial—it's where you begin to ease back into a more standard diet, but it's essential to proceed with caution to support your body's healing and maintain your health.

Here's how to navigate reintroducing foods safely:

1. **Gradually Broaden Your Diet:** Begin by adding one or two new foods to your diet daily. Yet, be mindful of items that might trigger bloating or gas, such as spicy foods, onions, broccoli, and those with a lot of peppers.
2. **Eat Mindfully:** Take time to chew your food well, which helps with digestion and lets you truly enjoy each flavor. Slow down your eating pace and introduce new foods slowly to prevent any digestive issues.
3. **Watch Your Portions:** Keep your meal sizes to about 1/3 cup. It's best not to exceed a cup per meal to avoid overburdening your digestive system and causing discomfort.
4. **Stay Hydrated the Right Way:** Follow the 30/30 rule—drink water 30 minutes before or after meals, but not during. Aim for 48 to 64 ounces of water daily, ideally sipped between meals to ensure you're well-hydrated without impacting your digestion.

Choosing What to Eat (and What to Skip)

As you start eating more familiar foods, some should remain off the menu:

- **Avoid:** Rice, bread, pasta, alcohol, dry meats, fruits with thick skins, fried foods, carbonated drinks, sugary foods, baked goods, and foods high in oils.
- **Good Choices:** Focus on easily digestible, high-protein foods like fish, skinless chicken, and turkey.
- **Be Cautious with Carbs:** You might crave grains, potatoes, or bread, but prioritize proteins and limit carbs and unhealthy fats.
- **Sauce and Condiments:** Limit high-fat sauces like mayonnaise and butter. Use other condiments sparingly, especially those high in sugar like ketchup, to avoid dumping syndrome.
- **Drinks:** Stick to water with meals to avoid digestion issues. Introducing other drinks can hinder the digestive process.

General Eating Recommendations:

- Aim for three to four meals a day, stopping once you're full or have reached a cup of food.
- Avoid snacks between meals. If you're hungry, wait for the next meal.
- To promote restful sleep, don't eat 2 to 3 hours before bedtime.

This period is your chance to slowly reintroduce a variety of foods while still paying close attention to how your body responds. With careful planning and selection, you're setting the stage for a well-balanced and healthful diet.

Stage 4 – Recipes

Part 1: Appetizers, Snacks & Sides

1. Crispy Baked Mozzarella Bites

Skill Level: ★★☆☆☆

Prep Duration: 15 mins

Cook Duration: 10 mins

Yield: 6 servings

Ingredients:

- 6 pieces of part-skim mozzarella string cheese, cut in half, for a gooey center.
- 1/2 cup of crushed high-fiber cereal, providing a crispy outer layer.
- 3 tbsp. of whole-wheat bread crumbs, for added texture.
- 3 tbsp. of low-fat grated parmesan cheese, adding a savory depth.
- 1/8 tsp. of salt-free Italian seasoning, for a hint of herbaceous flavor.
- 1/4 tsp. of onion powder, to subtly enhance the taste.
- 1 egg, lightly beaten, to help the coatings adhere.
- 1 tbsp. of water, to thin the egg wash.
- Salt & black pepper, to taste, for seasoning.

Directions:

1. Preheat your oven to 350°F (177°C) to ensure it's ready for baking.
2. Whisk together the egg and water in a small dish, creating an egg wash.
3. In another dish, combine the whole-wheat bread crumbs, crushed high-fiber cereal, low-fat grated parmesan cheese, Italian seasoning, and onion powder.
4. Dip each halved mozzarella string cheese first into the egg wash, ensuring it's fully coated.
5. Then, roll it in the breadcrumb mixture, pressing lightly to ensure the crumbs stick well.
6. Place the coated cheese halves on a baking tray lined with parchment paper.
7. Bake in the preheated oven for about 10 minutes, or until the cheese is bubbly and the coating turns golden.
8. Serve these crispy delights warm, paired with a zesty marinara sauce for dipping.

Nutrition Per Serving:

120 Kcal | 200 mg Sodium | 10 g Protein | 10 g Carbs | 6 g Fat | 100 mg Potassium

2. Mango & Avocado Salsa

Skill Level: ★☆☆☆☆

Prep Duration: 15 mins

Cook Duration: 0 mins

Yield: 4 servings

Ingredients:

- 1 ripe avocados, diced, for a creamy, rich base.
- ½ mango, cut into small chunks, adding sweetness and tropical flair.
- 1 garlic cloves, minced, for a punch of flavor.
- 2 tbsp of sliced green onion, for a mild, oniony crunch.
- ¼ jalapeno, chopped and seeds removed, for a gentle heat.
- ½ tsp. of ground cumin, for a warm, earthy spice.
- Juice of ½ lime, adding zest and brightness.
- 1 tbsp. of fresh cilantro, finely chopped, for a burst of herbal freshness.

- A pinch of sea salt and black pepper, for seasoning.
- A dash of cayenne pepper, for an extra spicy kick.

Directions:

1. In a large mixing bowl, gently combine the diced avocados, mango chunks, minced garlic, sliced green onion, chopped jalapeno, ground cumin, lime juice, and fresh cilantro.
2. Using a fork, lightly mash the mixture together, allowing some chunks to remain for texture. Season with sea salt, black pepper, and a dash of cayenne pepper to taste.
3. Serve the salsa immediately with tortilla chips for dipping or use it as a vibrant, flavorful topping for grilled fish or chicken.

Nutrition Per Serving:

90 Kcal | 40 mg Sodium | 1 g Protein | 6 g Carbs | 7 g Fat | 250 mg Potassium

3. Strawberry Protein Bliss Balls

Skill Level: ★★☆☆☆

Prep Duration: 10 mins

Refrigeration Duration: 3 hrs

Yield: 8 servings

Ingredients:

- 8 oz. of low-fat Greek yogurt cream cheese, providing a creamy base.
- ¼ cup of sugar-free strawberry jelly, for a touch of sweetness without the sugar.
- 2 scoops of protein powder, to add a protein punch.
- ½ tsp. of vanilla essence, for a hint of rich flavor.
- ¼ cup of no-calorie sweetener, keeping it sweet yet healthy.
- 1 cup of fresh strawberries, finely chopped, for fresh bursts of flavor.

Directions:

1. In a mixing bowl, whisk together the Greek yogurt cream cheese, protein powder, vanilla essence, and no-calorie sweetener until smooth.
2. Gently fold in the drained sugar-free strawberry jelly and finely chopped strawberries into the cream cheese mixture, ensuring even distribution without crushing the fruit.
3. Lay out a piece of plastic wrap on a flat surface. Transfer the mixture onto the plastic wrap, and use it to shape the mixture into a ball.
4. Place the protein delight ball in the refrigerator and let it set for 3 hours, ensuring it becomes firm and holds its shape.
5. Serve the strawberry protein bliss balls chilled, accompanied by biscuits or fresh fruit slices for dipping.

Nutrition Per Serving:

100 Kcal | 100 mg Sodium | 8 g Protein | 5 g Carbs | 4 g Fat | 150 mg Potassium

4. Artichoke & Zucchini Parmesan Rounds

Skill Level: ★★☆☆☆

Prep Duration: 15 mins

Cook Duration: 20 mins

Yield: 6 servings

Ingredients:

- 3 medium zucchinis, sliced into rounds, offering a fresh, mild base.
- 1 can (14 oz) of artichoke hearts, diced and drained, for a tangy, fibrous addition.
- 1 red bell peppers, diced, adding sweetness and color.
- 2 oz. of low-fat parmesan cheese, shredded, for a salty, cheesy topping.
- 1/4 cup of non-fat Greek yogurt, providing creaminess without the fat.
- 1 minced garlic cloves, for a punch of flavor.
- 1 tbsp. of Greek seasoning, to bring all the flavors together.

Directions:

1. Preheat your oven to 425°F (218°C) and line a baking sheet with parchment paper to prevent sticking.
2. Lay out the zucchini slices on the prepared baking sheet in a single layer, providing the perfect canvas for the toppings.

3. In a mixing bowl, stir together the diced artichoke hearts, red bell peppers, shredded low-fat parmesan cheese, non-fat Greek yogurt, minced garlic, and Greek seasoning until well combined. This mixture will be thick but spreadable.
4. Spoon the artichoke mixture onto each zucchini round, making sure each piece gets a generous portion of the topping.
5. Bake in the preheated oven for about 15 minutes, or until the topping is golden and bubbly, and the zucchini rounds are tender.
6. Serve the artichoke and zucchini parmesan rounds warm, enjoying the creamy, cheesy texture combined with the crispness of the zucchini.

Nutrition Per Serving:

60 Kcal | 200 mg Sodium | 5 g Protein | 5 g Carbs | 2.5 g Fat | 220 mg Potassium

5. Stuffed Swiss Cheese Mushrooms

Skill Level: ★☆☆☆☆

Prep Duration: 20 mins

Cook Duration: 10 mins

Yield: 4 servings

Ingredients:

- 8 medium-sized mushrooms, providing a natural, earthy vessel for stuffing.
- 1 pack of low-sodium beef bouillon cube, dissolved in ¼ cup hot water, for enriching the mushrooms with savory depth.
- 2 oz. of grated low-fat Swiss cheese, for a melty, creamy filling.

Directions:

1. Start by preheating your oven to 400°F (204°C) to ensure it's ready for baking.
2. Gently remove the stems from the mushrooms and chop them finely. This will be part of the filling, adding texture and flavor.
3. In a bowl, mix the chopped mushroom stems with the grated low-fat Swiss cheese, creating a cohesive stuffing.
4. Carefully hollow out the mushroom caps, creating a pocket that's perfect for filling.
5. Stuff each mushroom cap with a generous portion of the Swiss cheese mixture, ensuring it's well-packed.
6. Drizzle the prepared beef bouillon soup solution mixed with a little water over the stuffed mushrooms. This will add moisture and a burst of flavor as they cook.
7. Bake the mushrooms in the preheated oven for 7-10 minutes, or until the cheese has melted and the mushrooms are tender.
8. Serve the stuffed mushrooms hot, offering a delicious and nutritious appetizer or side dish.

Nutrition Per Serving:

60 Kcal | 125 mg Sodium | 6 g Protein | 4 g Carbs | 2.5 g Fat | 250 mg Potassium

6. Pumpkin Spice Chia Pudding

Skill Level: ★★☆☆☆

Prep Duration: 10 mins

Cook Duration: 0 hrs

Yield: 4 servings

Ingredients:

- ¼ cup of chia seeds, for a rich source of omega-3s and fiber.
- ½ cup of coconut milk (canned), adding a creamy texture and tropical flavor.
- ½ cup of pumpkin puree, for a seasonal touch and added nutrients.
- ½ cup of regular milk, to balance the thickness and add creaminess.
- 1 tsp of pumpkin seasoning, infusing the pudding with the warm flavors of autumn.
- 1 tsp of liquid stevia, for a touch of sweetness without added sugar.

Directions:

1. In a large mixing bowl, whisk together the chia seeds, coconut milk, pumpkin puree, regular milk, pumpkin seasoning, and liquid stevia until fully combined. This mixture will begin to thicken as it stands.
2. Evenly distribute the mixture into individual serving dishes or a large container if preferred.

3. Place the dishes or container in the refrigerator to chill. The pudding will continue to thicken and set as it cools, transforming into a delightfully creamy texture.
4. Serve the pudding cold, straight from the refrigerator, for a refreshing and nutritious dessert or snack.

Nutrition Per Serving: 90 Kcal | 40 mg Sodium | 4 g Protein | 12 g Carbs | 4 g Fat | 180 mg Potassium

7. Simple Chicken Soup Gravy

Skill Level: ★☆☆☆☆

Prep Duration: 10 mins

Cook Duration: 0 hrs

Yield: 4 servings

Ingredients:

- ½ cup of warm water, to dilute and smooth the gravy.
- 1 pack (10.5 oz) of low-sodium chicken soup cream, for a rich and flavorful base.

Directions:

1. In a medium-sized bowl, whisk together the warm water and low-sodium chicken soup cream until the mixture is completely smooth and well combined.
2. Serve the gravy immediately, perfect for drizzling over your favorite dishes to enhance their flavor with a comforting, chicken soup essence.

Nutrition Per Serving:

60 Kcal | 200 mg Sodium | 2 g Protein | 8 g Carbs | 2.5 g Fat | 50 mg Potassium

8. Caprese Salad Bites

Skill Level: ★★☆☆☆

Prep Duration: 10 mins

Cook Duration: 0 hrs

Yield: 4 servings

Ingredients:

- 11 cherry tomatoes, halved, for a juicy, tangy burst of flavor.
- 2 sticks of light mozzarella cheese, diced into 1" pieces, for a soft, creamy texture.
- 1 tsp of fresh basil, chopped, adding a fragrant, herby note.
- 1 tsp of olive oil, to bring all the flavors together with a smooth richness.
- 1 tsp of balsamic reduction, for a sweet and tangy glaze.
- ¼ tsp each of ground sea salt and black pepper, to enhance the salad's taste.

Directions:

1. In a large salad bowl, gently toss the halved cherry tomatoes with the diced mozzarella cheese and chopped fresh basil, ensuring a good mix of flavors in every bite.
2. Drizzle the olive oil and balsamic reduction over the tomato and mozzarella mixture, evenly coating the ingredients with the dressing.
3. Season with ground sea salt and black pepper, tossing the salad gently once more to distribute the seasonings throughout.
4. Serve the salad immediately, offering a refreshing and light dish that's perfect for any occasion.

Nutrition Per Serving:

60 Kcal | 70 mg Sodium | 6 g Protein | 2 g Carbs | 4 g Fat | 180 mg Potassium

9. Chicken Salad on Cucumber Slices

Skill Level: ★★☆☆☆

Prep Duration: 15 mins

Cook Duration: 0 hrs

Yield: 4 servings

Ingredients:

- 1 cooked chicken breast, chopped into bite-sized pieces, providing a lean protein base.
- 1 cucumber, sliced into rounds, offering a crisp, refreshing base.
- ¼ cup of light mayonnaise, adding creaminess with fewer calories.
- ¼ cup of finely chopped red onion, for a hint of sharpness and color.
- Salt and pepper, to taste, for seasoning.

Directions:

1. In a medium mixing bowl, combine the chopped chicken breast with the light mayonnaise and finely chopped red onion. Season the mixture with salt and pepper according to your taste preferences, ensuring all ingredients are well incorporated.
2. Place a spoonful of the chicken salad mixture on top of each cucumber slice, creating a neat, appetizing assembly.
3. Serve these bites immediately, offering a refreshing, protein-packed appetizer or snack that's perfect for gatherings or as a light, healthy meal option.

Nutrition Per Serving:

80 Kcal | 180 mg Sodium | 14 g Protein | 2 g Carbs | 3 g Fat | 160 mg Potassium

10. Baked Crispy Zucchini Chips

Skill Level: ★★☆☆☆

Prep Duration: 10 mins

Cook Duration: 2 hrs

Yield: 4 servings

Ingredients:

- 1 large zucchini, sliced thinly, for a light and healthy snack base.
- 1 tbsp olive oil, for brushing the slices to ensure crispiness.
- Kosher salt, to taste, for seasoning.

Directions:

1. Begin by preheating your oven to 225°F (107°C) to ensure a slow and even baking process.
2. Line two baking trays with parchment paper to prevent sticking and for easy cleanup.
3. Arrange the thinly sliced zucchini in a single layer on the prepared trays, avoiding overlap to ensure even baking.
4. Lightly brush each zucchini slice with olive oil. This helps in crisping up the slices and adds a subtle flavor.
5. Sprinkle the slices with kosher salt according to your taste preferences.
6. Place the trays in the preheated oven and bake for about 2 hours, or until the zucchini slices are crispy.
7. Let the zucchini chips cool before serving to allow them to crisp up further.

Nutrition Per Serving:

30 Kcal | 55 mg Sodium | 1 g Protein | 2 g Carbs | 2 g Fat | 150 mg Potassium

11. Creamy Cauliflower Mash with Chicken Flavor

Skill Level: ★★☆☆☆

Prep Duration: 20 mins

Cook Duration: 20 mins

Yield: 4 servings

Ingredients:

- 16 oz. of cauliflower florets, fresh or previously frozen, as the base.
- 1 pack (10.5 oz) of low-sodium chicken soup cream, to infuse a savory chicken flavor.

Directions:

1. Bring a pot of water to a boil and add the cauliflower florets. Cook them until they become very soft, which is essential for achieving a smooth, creamy texture.
2. Once the cauliflower is soft, drain the water and transfer the florets to a mixing bowl. Use a potato masher or an electric mixer to mash the cauliflower thoroughly until no large chunks remain.
3. Gradually mix in half of the chicken soup cream pack into the mashed cauliflower. Continue to blend until the mixture is well-combined and smooth.
4. Taste the cauliflower mash and adjust the seasoning if necessary. The chicken soup cream should provide a flavorful base, but additional salt and pepper can be added as per your preference.
5. Serve the creamy cauliflower mash immediately, enjoying the rich, comforting taste enhanced by the savory notes of chicken.

Nutrition Per Serving:

70 Kcal | 260 mg Sodium | 3 g Protein | 10 g Carbs | 2 g Fat | 180 mg Potassium

12. Almond Mozzarella Pretzel Bites

Skill Level: ★★☆☆☆

Prep Duration: 25 mins

Cook Duration: 12 mins

Yield: 8 servings

Ingredients:

- 2.5 tbsp. of lukewarm water, to activate the yeast.
- 1 egg, beaten, to add richness and help bind the dough.
- 1 cup of ground almonds, for a gluten-free flour alternative.
- 1 ¼ cups of part-skim Mozzarella cheese, adding chewiness and flavor.
- 1 tbsp. of butter for brushing, to give a golden finish.
- 1 tsp. of plant fiber powder, to improve dough texture.
- 1 tsp. of active dry yeast, for leavening.
- 1 tsp. of a rising agent, to ensure the dough puffs up nicely.
- ½ tsp. of sea salt, for seasoning.
- 1 oz. of whipped cream cheese, for a creamy dough consistency.

Directions:

1. Start by preheating your oven to 430°F (220°C) to ensure it's ready for baking.
2. In a small bowl, dissolve the yeast in lukewarm water and allow it to sit for about 7 minutes, or until frothy, signaling that the yeast is active.
3. In a separate bowl, mix together the ground almonds, plant fiber powder, rising agent, and half of the sea salt.
4. In a microwave-safe bowl, combine the Mozzarella and cream cheese. Microwave in short bursts, stirring between each, until the cheeses are completely melted and smooth.
5. Add the yeast mixture to the melted cheese mixture, stirring to combine.
6. Mix in the beaten egg to the cheese and yeast mixture, then gradually incorporate the dry ingredients, kneading until a pliable dough forms.
7. Divide the dough and shape each piece into small pretzel bites. This portion size is perfect for snacking or sharing.
8. Place the pretzel bites on a baking tray lined with parchment paper and bake for about 12 minutes, or until they are golden brown.
9. Right out of the oven, brush the pretzel bites with butter and sprinkle the remaining sea salt over them for a classic pretzel flavor.
10. Serve the pretzel bites warm, offering a delicious, gluten-free snack that's both satisfying and creative.

Nutrition Per 2 Pretzels:

120 Kcal | 180 mg Sodium | 7 g Protein | 3 g Carbs | 10 g Fat | 70 mg Potassium

13. Divine Chicken Salad Spread

Skill Level: ★★☆☆☆

Prep Duration: 15 mins

Cook Duration: 0 mins

Yield: 2 servings

Ingredients:

- A blend of seasoning mix (onion salt, pepper, and garlic granules), adjusted to your taste, for a savory kick.
- 3.5 tbsp. of zero-fat Greek yogurt, for creaminess without the guilt.
- 3-5 quartered cherry tomatoes, adding a fresh, juicy element.
- 2.5 tbsp. of light mayonnaise, ensuring a rich texture with fewer calories.
- 1 small can of canned chicken chunks, for convenience and protein.
- 1.5 tbsp. of chopped onion, for a sharp, aromatic crunch.

Directions:

1. Start by pulling apart the canned chicken chunks into smaller pieces, making them easier to mix and eat.

2. Add the chopped onions to the chicken, combining them for a base of flavor.
3. Stir in the zero-fat Greek yogurt, light mayonnaise, quartered cherry tomatoes, and the blend of seasoning mix. Mix thoroughly until all ingredients are well incorporated and the mixture is creamy.
4. Taste and adjust the seasoning as needed, ensuring the spread has the perfect balance of savory, creamy, and fresh flavors.
5. Serve the chicken salad spread as a delightful dip with crackers or as a spread on whole-grain bread for a satisfying meal.

Nutrition Per Serving:

80 Kcal | 150 mg Sodium | 14 g Protein | 3 g Carbs | 2 g Fat | 70 mg Potassium

14. Spicy Pinto Bean Dip

Skill Level: ★★☆☆☆

Prep Duration: 20 mins

Cook Duration: 12 mins

Yield: 8 servings

Ingredients:

- 2 garlic cloves, crushed, for a robust flavor foundation.
- ¼ tsp. of crushed red pepper, adding a heat that tickles the palate.
- ¼ cup of water, to assist in blending and achieving the right consistency.
- 1 can (15 oz.) of drained Pinto beans, the star ingredient for a hearty texture.
- 1 tsp. of cumin powder, for a warm, earthy undertone.
- ½ tsp. of chili seasoning, to infuse the dip with a spicy kick.
- ½ cup of low-fat blended cheese, for creamy, melty goodness.
- ¼ cup of light sour cream, adding a tangy richness.
- Seasoning: Salt & pepper, adjusted to taste, for perfect seasoning.
- ¼ cup of reduced-fat whipped cream cheese, for extra creaminess and flavor.

Directions:

1. In a blender, combine the water, crushed garlic, and Pinto beans. Blend until a coarse paste is achieved, creating a textured base for the dip.
2. Transfer the bean mixture to a skillet and cook over medium heat with cumin powder and chili seasoning, stirring frequently to prevent sticking and ensure even flavor distribution.
3. Once the bean mixture is fragrant and heated through, incorporate the light sour cream, whipped cream cheese, and half of the blended cheese. Continue to stir until all ingredients are well combined and the mixture is smooth.
4. Move the bean dip to a serving dish. Sprinkle the remaining half of the blended cheese evenly over the top.
5. Briefly melt the cheese in the microwave, watching closely to avoid overheating. This step ensures a gooey, inviting top layer.
6. Serve the dip warm, perfect as a hearty snack or a flavorful addition to any meal.

Nutrition Per Serving:

100 Kcal | 150 mg Sodium | 5 g Protein | 10 g Carbs | 3 g Fat | 150 mg Potassium

15. Savory Pinto Bean Dip

Skill Level: ★★☆☆☆

Prep Duration: 20 mins

Cook Duration: 12 mins

Yield: 8 servings

Ingredients:

- 2 crushed garlic cloves, for a robust flavor base.
- ¼ tsp. of crushed red pepper, adding a touch of heat.
- ¼ cup of water, to help blend the beans into a smooth paste.
- 1 can (15 oz.) of drained Pinto beans, the main ingredient for a hearty texture and taste.
- 1 tsp. of cumin powder, providing a warm, earthy note.
- Half tsp. of chili seasoning, for a hint of smoky spice.
- ½ cup of low-fat blended cheese, for gooey deliciousness with fewer calories.

- ¼ cup of light sour cream, for a tangy creaminess.
- Seasoning: Salt & pepper, to enhance all the flavors.
- ¼ cup of reduced-fat whipped cream cheese, adding richness without the guilt.

Directions:

1. Begin by blending together the water, garlic, and Pinto beans until a coarse paste is achieved. This mixture will form the foundation of your dip.
2. Transfer the bean paste to a skillet and cook it over medium heat with the cumin powder and chili seasoning, stirring regularly.
3. Gradually mix in the light sour cream, reduced-fat whipped cream cheese, and half of the low-fat blended cheese until the mixture is well combined and creamy.
4. Once the dip is thoroughly mixed, move it to a serving dish. Sprinkle the remaining cheese evenly over the top.
5. Briefly melt the cheese in a microwave, just until it's perfectly gooey and ready to serve.

Nutrition Per Serving:

100 Kcal | 150 mg Sodium | 5 g Protein | 10 g Carbs | 3 g Fat | 150 mg Potassium

Part 2: Meat & Poultry Recipes

1. Hearty Pumpkin & Chicken Bake

Skill Level: ★★☆☆☆

Prep Duration: 30 mins

Cook Duration: 1 hr

Yield: 4 servings

Ingredients:

- 2/3 cup of breadcrumbs, for a crunchy topping.
- 1 can (10.5 oz) of creamy poultry broth (reduced-fat), providing a rich base without the extra calories.
- 1 cup of cubed sweet pumpkin, adding sweetness and texture.
- ½ cup of semi-skimmed milk, to create a creamy texture with less fat.
- 1 pound of minced chicken, for lean protein.
- 1 apple, chopped, for a hint of sweetness and moisture.
- ½ cup of reduced-fat mozzarella, grated, for cheesy goodness with fewer calories.

Directions:

1. Preheat your oven to 350°F (175°C) to get it ready for baking.
2. In a skillet, cook the minced chicken until it's fully cooked through, ensuring there's no pink left in the meat.
3. Stir in the semi-skimmed milk and creamy poultry broth into the cooked chicken, and bring the mixture to a simmer.
4. Add the cubed sweet pumpkin and chopped apple to the skillet, and let it simmer for another 12-17 minutes, allowing the flavors to meld and the pumpkin to soften.
5. Transfer the chicken and pumpkin mixture into an ovenproof dish. Evenly sprinkle the breadcrumbs and grated reduced-fat mozzarella cheese over the top, creating a layer for texture and flavor.
6. Bake in the preheated oven for about 12 minutes, or until the breadcrumb and cheese topping is golden and bubbly.
7. Enjoy the dish warm, savoring the combination of savory chicken, sweet pumpkin, and the creamy, crunchy topping.

Nutrition Per Serving:

210 Kcal | 250 mg Sodium | 23 g Protein | 12 g Carbs | 8 g Fat | 350 mg Potassium

2. Tangerine-Infused Chicken Fennel Pouches

Skill Level: ★★☆☆☆

Prep Duration: 20 mins

Cook Duration: 25 mins

Yield: 1 serving

Ingredients:

- ½ fennel bulb, finely sliced, for a crunchy, anise-like sweetness.
- 4 oz lean chicken breast strips, ready for flavor infusion.

- 1 tbsp. of fresh parsley, minced, for a burst of freshness.
- ½ tsp. of zesty pepper seasoning, adding a vibrant kick.
- ½ tbsp. of sunflower oil, for a light, non-overpowering fat source.
- ½ tangerine, sliced, for a citrusy, sweet tang.

Directions:

1. Preheat your oven to 355°F (180°C), setting it up for a gentle, even cooking process.
2. Cut four sheets of aluminum foil into 13 by 13-inch squares, preparing them for the pouches.
3. Lay out the chicken strips on each foil sheet. Drizzle each with sunflower oil and evenly sprinkle with the zesty pepper seasoning for a perfectly coated flavor base.
4. Garnish the chicken with the tangerine segments, adding a layer of citrus sweetness. Scatter the finely sliced fennel and minced parsley over the top, introducing a fresh, aromatic depth.
5. Carefully fold and seal each aluminum foil sheet, creating secure packets that will steam the ingredients inside, locking in the flavors and moisture.
6. Bake the packets in the preheated oven for about 19-22 minutes. The steam within will gently cook the chicken, fennel, and tangerine, merging their flavors.
7. Serve the packets hot, allowing the steam and aromas to escape as they're opened, presenting a perfectly cooked, fragrant dish.

Nutrition Per Serving:

120 Kcal | 80 mg Sodium | 15 g Protein | 4 g Carbs | 5 g Fat | 250 mg Potassium

3. Sweet & Savory Beef Kabobs

Skill Level: ★★☆☆☆

Prep Duration: 20 mins

Cook Duration: 25 mins

Yield: 1 serving

Ingredients:

- 1 tbsp. of apple cider vinegar, for a tangy marinade base.
- ¼ cup of chopped shallots, adding a mild, sweet flavor.
- 1 garlic bud, crushed, for a punch of aroma.
- 1 tbsp. of soy sauce, contributing saltiness and depth.
- 4 oz. of prime beef, cubed, as the protein star of the dish.
- 6 grape tomatoes, for bursts of juiciness.
- ¼ cup of sliced yellow bell pepper, adding sweetness and crunch.
- ¼ cup of honeydew melon bits, for an unexpected sweetness.
- 3 button mushrooms, quartered, for earthiness.
- ½ tbsp. of vegetable oil, to help the veggies grill nicely.

Directions:

1. In a bowl, whisk together the garlic, soy sauce, apple cider vinegar, and shallots. Add the beef cubes to this marinade, ensuring they are fully coated. Let the beef marinate for 17 minutes to absorb the flavors deeply.
2. Preheat your oven to 380°F (193°C) or prepare your grill if you prefer outdoor cooking.
3. In a separate bowl, toss the vegetables and honeydew melon bits with the vegetable oil, ensuring they are lightly coated.
4. Carefully thread the marinated beef, grape tomatoes, yellow bell pepper slices, honeydew melon bits, and quartered button mushrooms onto pre-soaked skewers, alternating for color and flavor variety.
5. Grill the skewers for about 23 minutes, turning them midway to ensure even cooking and a beautiful char on all sides.

Nutrition Per Serving:

180 Kcal | 200 mg Sodium | 20 g Protein | 10 g Carbs | 6 g Fat | 350 mg Potassium

4. Zesty Chicken Fajita Bowl

Skill Level: ★★☆☆☆

Prep Duration: 15 mins

Cook Duration: 25 mins

Yield: 2 servings

Ingredients: For the Chicken:

- ¾ tsp. smoked paprika, for a deep, smoky flavor.
- ½ lb (8 oz) of chicken slices, lean and ready for marinating.
- ½ tsp. herbal salt, to enhance flavor naturally.
- Juice of ¼ lemon, adding a tangy zest.
- 1 tbsp. tomato sauce, for a hint of sweetness and richness.
- 1 tbsp. olive oil, for cooking and marinating.

For the Veggies:

- ½ tsp. herbal salt, for seasoning.
- ½ brown onion, segmented, for a savory foundation.
- 1 each of ruby, amber, and emerald bell peppers, segmented, for a colorful veggie mix.
- 1/2 tsp. coriander, for a fresh, citrusy note.
- 1 tbsp. olive oil, for sautéing.
- 2 cups cooked broccoli rice, as a nutritious, low-carb base.

Directions:

1. Combine smoked paprika, herbal salt, lemon juice, tomato sauce, and olive oil in a bowl, excluding the chicken. Once the marinade is blended, coat the chicken slices thoroughly.
2. Heat olive oil in a skillet over a medium-high flame. Sauté the onions until they're translucent, then add the bell peppers, herbal salt, and coriander. Cook for about 5 minutes, until the veggies are tender yet crisp.
3. In another skillet, grill the marinated chicken for approximately 5 minutes on each side, ensuring it's well-cooked and flavorful.
4. Assemble the bowls by first laying down a base of broccoli rice, then topping with the sautéed veggies and grilled chicken slices.

Nutrition Per Serving: 240 Kcal | 130 mg Sodium | 21 g Protein | 10 g Carbs | 12 g Fat | 275 mg Potassium

5. Robust Venison & Bean Chili

Skill Level: ★★☆☆☆

Prep Duration: 12 mins

Cook Duration: 55 mins

Yield: 4 servings

Ingredients:

- 4 cups of liquid (water or broth), adjusted as needed to cover the beans and meat.
- 1 shallots, finely chopped, for a subtle, sweet flavor base.
- ½ pounds of ground venison, offering a rich, lean protein source.
- 1 cup of dry pinto beans, rinsed and cleaned, for hearty, fiber-rich bulk.
- 1 tbsp. of olive oil, for sautéing the ingredients.
- 1 garlic pods, finely chopped, adding aromatic depth.
- 1 tbsp. of basil, for herbal freshness.
- 1 can (15 oz) of preserved diced tomatoes, providing moisture and tanginess.
- ½ yellow bell pepper, segmented, for a sweet crunch.
- ½ cup of tomato puree, to intensify the tomato flavor.
- Salt & pepper to taste, for seasoning.
- 1 tsp of cayenne pepper, offering a spicy kick.
- 2 cups of meat broth, enriching the chili with savory depth.
- 1 tsp of toasted coriander, adding a warm, citrusy note.

Directions:

1. Start by adding the dry pinto beans to a pressure cooker, covering them with the liquid. Cook on high for 23 minutes to soften the beans quickly.
2. After cooking, drain the beans and set aside. Clean the pressure cooker for the next steps.
3. Heat the olive oil in the pressure cooker and sauté the garlic, ground venison, yellow bell pepper, and shallots until golden-brown and fully cooked.
4. Combine the sautéed meat mixture with the pre-cooked beans. Add the preserved diced tomatoes, tomato puree, meat broth, and the

rest of the spices, stirring well to incorporate all the ingredients.

5. Cook the mixture on high for another 35 minutes, allowing the flavors to meld and the chili to thicken. Allow the pressure to release naturally before opening the cooker.
6. Serve the hearty meat chili hot, garnished with additional fresh herbs if desired, for a comforting, protein-packed meal.

Nutrition Per Serving:

280 Kcal | 300 mg Sodium | 31 g Protein | 18 g Carbs | 8 g Fat | 406 mg Potassium

6. Southwest Chicken Bites

Skill Level: ★★☆☆☆

Prep Duration: 20 mins

Cook Duration: 20 mins

Yield: 12 servings

Ingredients:

- 1 small jalapeño, deseeded for a spicy kick without overwhelming heat.
- 1/2 of a bell pepper, diced, adding sweetness and crunch.
- 1/4 cup breadcrumbs, for binding and a slight crunch.
- 2 garlic cloves, minced, to infuse a robust flavor.
- A touch of dried basil, for an aromatic herbiness.
- 1.5 lbs of ground chicken, providing a lean protein base.
- 3 green onions, chopped, for a mild onion flavor.
- 1 large egg, helping to bind the mixture together.
- 1/4 tsp white pepper, for a subtle spiciness.
- 1 tsp paprika, adding a smoky undertone.
- 1/4 cup fresh parsley, chopped, for freshness and color.
- 1/2 tsp rock salt, to enhance all the flavors.

Directions:

1. Start by preheating your oven to 400°F (200°C), preparing it for baking.
2. Use a blender to finely chop the green onions, jalapeño, parsley, bell pepper, and garlic, ensuring a uniform distribution of flavors.
3. In a large mixing bowl, combine the blended vegetable mixture with the ground chicken, breadcrumbs, egg, white pepper, paprika, dried basil, and rock salt. Mix thoroughly until all ingredients are well incorporated.
4. Shape the mixture into small, bite-sized balls and arrange them on a baking tray lined with parchment paper. This helps in easy removal post-baking and minimal cleanup.
5. Bake in the preheated oven for 15-20 minutes, or until the chicken bites are golden brown and cooked through. The high heat ensures a crispy exterior while keeping the inside moist and flavorful.
6. Serve the baked chicken bites warm, perfect as an appetizer, snack, or part of a meal. They're sure to be a hit with their bold Southwest flavors.

Nutrition Per Serving:

70 Kcal | 150 mg Sodium | 10 g Protein | 2 g Carbs | 2 g Fat | 150 mg Potassium

7. Caprese-Inspired Chicken Fillets

Skill Level: ★★☆☆☆

Prep Duration: 15 mins

Cook Duration: 30 mins

Yield: 4 servings

Ingredients:

- 4 oz of mozzarella cheese, sliced thinly, adding creamy, melty delight.
- 1 tbsp of extra virgin olive oil, for richness and a smooth finish.
- 2 medium tomatoes, sliced into rounds, for a fresh, juicy contrast.
- 4 chicken fillets, 4 oz each, serving as a tender, protein-packed base.
- Salt & black pepper, to season, enhancing the natural flavors of the ingredients.
- 1/4 cup of fresh basil leaves, torn, infusing the dish with a fragrant, herbaceous note.

- 1 tbsp of aged balsamic reduction, drizzled for a sweet and tangy glaze.

Directions:

1. Begin by preheating your oven to 400°F (200°C), setting up for a thorough cook.
2. Make careful slits in each chicken fillet, deep enough to hold the fillings but not so much that you cut through completely.
3. Generously season each fillet with salt and pepper. Neatly tuck slices of mozzarella, basil leaves, and tomato rounds into the slits, distributing them evenly for balanced flavor in every bite.
4. Lay the stuffed fillets on a baking tray. Drizzle them with the extra virgin olive oil and aged balsamic reduction, ensuring each fillet is lightly coated for added flavor and moisture.
5. Place the tray in the preheated oven, baking for 25-30 minutes, or until the chicken is fully cooked and the cheese has melted beautifully.
6. Serve the fillets hot, ideally as they come out of the oven, to enjoy the full, vibrant flavors of the basil, mozzarella, and tomato in harmony with the juicy chicken.

Nutrition Per Serving:

260 Kcal | 150 mg Sodium | 36 g Protein | 3 g Carbs | 11 g Fat | 450 mg Potassium

8. Mediterranean Chicken and Vegetable Harmony

Skill Level: ★★☆☆☆

Prep Duration: 15 mins

Cook Duration: 25 mins

Yield: 4 servings

Ingredients:

- 4 cups of your favorite vegetables, cut into bite-sized pieces. Think colorful peppers, zucchini, cherry tomatoes, and eggplants for a Mediterranean twist.
- 12 oz of chicken breast, trimmed and ready for seasoning. A lean, healthy protein source that's perfect for a light yet satisfying dish.
- 2 tbsp of extra virgin olive oil, rich in flavor and heart-healthy fats, divided for marinating the chicken and tossing the vegetables.
- A blend of seasoning: sea salt, freshly ground black pepper, and a dash of garlic powder, to enhance the natural flavors of the chicken and vegetables.

Directions:

1. Start by preheating your oven to 400°F (200°C), getting it ready for a roasted delight.
2. Take the chicken breast and lovingly coat it in half the olive oil, seasoned generously with your salt, black pepper, and garlic powder blend. This ensures the chicken is flavorful and moist.
3. Arrange the chicken on a baking sheet and let it roast in the oven for 20 minutes, or until it reaches a safe internal temperature and is beautifully golden.
4. While the chicken is roasting, steam your selection of vegetables until they're just al dente. You want them tender yet slightly crisp for that perfect texture contrast.
5. Once the vegetables are steamed to perfection, toss them in the remaining olive oil and a sprinkle of the seasoning blend, making sure they're well-coated and flavorful.
6. Serve the succulent chicken alongside the vibrant vegetable medley for a meal that's not only nourishing but also a feast for the eyes.

Nutrition Per Serving:

215 Kcal | 115 mg Sodium | 14 g Protein | 5 g Carbs | 9 g Fat | 315 mg Potassium

9. Turkey and Cauliflower Stuffed Cabbage Rolls

Skill Level: ★★☆☆☆

Prep Duration: 15 mins

Cook Duration: 35 mins

Yield: 12 servings

Ingredients:

- 1 lb lean ground turkey, providing a high-protein filling.
- 2 tbsp paprika blend, for a smoky, sweet depth of flavor.

- 1 cup cauliflower florets, adding a nutritious crunch.
- 1 medium onion, finely chopped, for a base layer of flavor.
- 1/2 tsp garlic seasoning, for aromatic warmth.
- 1/4 tsp each of salt and pepper, to season.
- 12 large cabbage leaves, used as the wrap for the filling.
- 10 oz diced tomatoes (no salt added), for a fresh, tangy sauce.
- 1/2 tsp Mediterranean herbs blend, to bring the flavors of the region.
- 1 tsp sugar substitute, to balance the acidity of the tomatoes.
- 2 tbsp umami sauce, for a depth of savory flavor.
- 1/2 tsp onion essence, to enhance the oniony sweetness.

Directions:

1. Preheat the oven to 350°F (175°C) to ensure it's ready for baking.
2. Boil the cabbage leaves for 5 minutes until they become pliable, then carefully drain them and set aside.
3. Heat a bit of oil in a skillet over medium heat. Sauté the chopped onions until they are translucent, then add the ground turkey. Cook until the turkey is no longer pink.
4. Stir in the paprika blend, Mediterranean herbs, half of the garlic seasoning, umami sauce, and onion essence into the turkey. Add the cauliflower florets and cook for an additional 2 minutes, allowing the flavors to meld.
5. In a food processor, blend the diced tomatoes with the remaining garlic and onion seasoning to create a smooth sauce.
6. Lay out the softened cabbage leaves and place approximately 2 oz of the turkey mixture onto each leaf. Roll them up tightly and place them seam side down in a baking dish.
7. Pour the blended tomato sauce over the cabbage rolls, covering them evenly.
8. Bake in the preheated oven for 25 minutes, until the cabbage is tender and the filling is hot.
9. Serve the cabbage rolls warm, enjoying the savory filling encased in the soft, sweet cabbage leaves.

Nutrition Per Serving:

105 Kcal | 60 mg Sodium | 7.5 g Protein | 4.5 g Carbs | 5 g Fat | 175 mg Potassium

10. Tender Slow-Cooked Pork Tacos

Skill Level: ★★☆☆☆

Prep Duration: 20 mins

Cook Duration: 2 hrs

Yield: 12 servings

Ingredients:

- 2 tbsp spicy seasoning mix, for a robust flavor.
- 4 garlic cloves, mashed, infusing a bold aroma.
- 2 tbsp vegetable oil, for searing the pork.
- 2 lbs boneless pork loin, the star of your taco filling.
- 1 cup white onion, finely diced, adding a sweet crunch.
- 12 small corn tortillas, providing the perfect vessel.
- 1 cup vegetable broth, creating a moist cooking environment.
- 2 tpsp lemon juice, for a tangy twist.
- 1/2 cup tart cherry juice, introducing a unique, sweet and sour flavor profile.

Directions:

1. Preheat your oven to 350°F (177°C) to get it ready for slow cooking.
2. Generously rub the pork loin with the spicy seasoning mix to ensure every bite is packed with flavor.
3. In a Dutch oven or a similar heavy pot, heat the vegetable oil over medium-high. Sear the pork loin on each side until it's nicely browned, then set it aside.
4. In the same pot, sauté the onions until translucent. Add the mashed garlic towards the end to avoid burning, just long enough to release its fragrance.
5. Pour in the vegetable broth and both the lemon and tart cherry juices, stirring to combine.

Return the pork to the pot, ensuring it's nestled in the liquid for even cooking.

6. Cover the pot with a lid and transfer it to the oven. Let the pork stew in the aromatic broth for about 90 minutes.
7. After 90 minutes, remove the lid to allow the top of the pork to brown and the sauce to thicken, continuing to cook for another 30 minutes.
8. Once cooked, shred the pork with two forks and serve it atop warmed corn tortillas. Garnish with your choice of toppings, such as diced onions, cilantro, or a squeeze of lime, for an extra layer of flavor.

Nutrition Per Serving:

150 Kcal | 105 mg Sodium | 16 g Protein | 8 g Carbs | 6 g Fat | 185 mg Potassium

11. Herbaceous Chicken with Tomato-Spinach Ragout

Skill Level: ★★☆☆☆

Prep Duration: 15 mins

Cook Duration: 25 mins

Yield: 6 servings

Ingredients:

- 1.5 pounds of chicken breast, cut into bite-sized pieces, for a lean protein base.
- 15 oz. can of diced tomatoes, providing a juicy, tangy foundation.
- 2 cloves of garlic, finely chopped, to add aromatic depth.
- 1 tbsp. of extra virgin olive oil, for sautéing and flavor enhancement.
- 8 oz. of fresh mushrooms, thinly sliced, for earthy notes.
- 5 oz. of fresh baby spinach, adding a pop of color and nutrition.
- Salt and pepper, for seasoning to taste.

Directions:

1. Heat the extra virgin olive oil in a large pan over medium heat, preparing it for the cooking process.
2. Add the chopped garlic to the pan, allowing it to sizzle until fragrant. Then, introduce the chicken pieces, sprinkling them with salt and pepper for seasoning.
3. Sauté the chicken until it turns a whitish color, indicating it's partially cooked.
4. Stir in the sliced mushrooms and the canned diced tomatoes, and continue cooking until the mushrooms become tender.
5. Finally, fold in the baby spinach and cook just until it wilts, integrating beautifully with the chicken and tomato mixture.
6. Adjust the seasoning with additional salt and pepper if necessary, ensuring a perfect balance of flavors.
7. Serve the dish warm, inviting everyone to enjoy the robust and herbaceous flavors of this delightful chicken meal.

Nutrition Per Serving:

130 Kcal | 140 mg Sodium | 27 g Protein | 5 g Carbs | 3 g Fat | 250 mg Potassium

12. Savory Chicken with Tomato-Spinach Sauce

Skill Level: ★★☆☆☆

Prep Duration: 15 mins

Cook Duration: 25 mins

Yield: 6 servings

Ingredients:

- 1.5 pounds chicken breast, cut into bite-size pieces for easy cooking and eating.
- 15 oz can of diced tomatoes, bringing a tangy and juicy element to the dish.
- 2 cloves of garlic, finely chopped, to infuse the sauce with aromatic depth.
- 1 tbsp extra virgin olive oil, for sautéing and adding richness.
- 8 oz fresh mushrooms, thinly sliced, to add earthy flavors and textures.
- 5 oz fresh baby spinach, for a touch of green and a boost of nutrition.
- Season with salt and pepper to taste, enhancing the natural flavors.

Directions:

1. Heat the olive oil in a skillet over medium heat. Add the garlic, then the chicken pieces, seasoning them with salt and pepper. Sauté until the chicken turns white, ensuring it's cooked evenly.
2. Add the mushrooms and canned tomatoes to the skillet, letting the mixture cook until the mushrooms are tender.
3. Gently fold in the baby spinach and cook just until it wilts. This adds a fresh, leafy texture and enriches the dish with vitamins.
4. Taste the sauce and adjust the seasoning with more salt and pepper if needed.
5. Serve the chicken hot, ensuring each plate is filled with a generous helping of the tomato-spinach sauce.

Nutrition Per Serving:

140 Kcal | 140 mg Sodium | 27 g Protein | 6 g Carbs | 4 g Fat | 320 mg Potassium

13. Creamy Chicken and Cauliflower Casserole

Skill Level: ★★☆☆☆

Prep Duration: 20 mins

Cook Duration: 40 mins

Yield: 7 servings

Ingredients:

- 2 boneless, skinless chicken breasts, halved and shredded, offering lean protein.
- 3 cups riced cauliflower, providing a healthy, low-carb alternative to grains.
- 1 tbsp. butter, for richness and flavor.
- 3 tsp. arrowroot powder dissolved in 6 tsp. of water, to thicken the sauce without flour.
- 1.5 cups chicken broth, adding depth and moisture.
- ½ cup sour cream, for a tangy, creamy texture.
- 1 cups grated Colby-jack cheese, offering a smooth melt and a touch of sharpness.
- 4 oz. chopped green chilies, for a mild kick.
- Spices: kosher salt, oregano, and chipotle chili powder, to season and add layers of flavor.

Directions:

1. Preheat the oven to 350°F. Melt butter in a large skillet over medium heat.
2. Stir in the arrowroot mixture and then slowly add the chicken broth, whisking until the sauce thickens.
3. Season with kosher salt, oregano, and chipotle chili powder, then let the mixture simmer for a minute to fuse the flavors.
4. Add the shredded chicken and riced cauliflower to the skillet, stirring well to combine.
5. Mix in the sour cream until the sauce becomes smooth and creamy.
6. Let the mixture simmer for a few minutes, then sprinkle the grated Colby-jack cheese over the top.
7. Transfer the skillet to the preheated oven and bake until the cheese has melted and the casserole is bubbly, about 20 minutes.
8. Serve hot, garnished with additional herbs or spices if desired.

Nutrition Per Serving:

180 Kcal | 160 mg Sodium | 20 g Protein | 8 g Carbs | 8 g Fat | 280 mg Potassium

14. Citrus-Infused Chicken with Spinach

Skill Level: ★★☆☆☆

Prep Duration: 20 mins

Cook Duration: 1 hr

Yield: 4 servings

Ingredients:

- 2 chicken breasts, boneless & skinless, cubed for quick cooking.
- 1 cup fresh orange juice, to marinate and infuse the chicken with bright citrus flavors.
- 1/2 cup chicken broth, adding depth to the sauce.
- 1 tbsp. honey, for natural sweetness to balance the citrus.
- 1 tbsp. toasted sesame oil, for sautéing and adding a nutty flavor.
- 1 tbsp. fresh ginger, grated, for a spicy, warm note.

- 1 tsp. garlic powder, for a robust flavor base.
- 1 tbsp. orange zest, to intensify the citrus profile.
- 2 cups coconut aminos, for a soy-free seasoning alternative.
- Steamed green beans, to serve as a fresh, crunchy side.
- Season with pepper to taste, for a spicy kick.

Directions:

1. Heat the sesame oil in a skillet over medium heat. Add the cubed chicken, seasoning lightly with pepper, and brown until cooked through. Remove and set aside.
2. In the same skillet, combine the fresh orange juice, chicken broth, honey, grated ginger, garlic powder, orange zest, and coconut aminos. Bring to a simmer and let the sauce thicken.
3. Return the chicken to the skillet, tossing it in the sauce to coat thoroughly.
4. Serve the citrus-infused chicken over a bed of steamed green beans or your choice of sides, enjoying the harmony of flavors.

Nutrition Per Serving:

200 Kcal | Sodium 120 mg | Protein 25 g | Carbs 15 g | Fat 7 g | Potassium: 300 mg

15. Asian-Inspired Chicken Lettuce Wraps

Skill Level: ★★☆☆☆

Prep Duration: 20 mins

Cook Duration: 50 mins

Yield: 4 servings

Ingredients:

- 1/2 pound ground chicken breast, for a light and lean filling.
- 8 small butter lettuce leaves, crisp and fresh, perfect for wrapping.
- 1/2 cup minced onion, adding a sweet depth of flavor.
- 1 tbsp. minced garlic, for a pungent kick.
- 1 tsp. minced ginger, bringing a spicy warmth.
- 1/2 can (4 oz.) water chestnuts, finely chopped, for a satisfying crunch.
- 1/2 cucumber, deseeded and sliced into strips, for a fresh, juicy crunch.
- 1 chopped scallion, for a sharp, green accent.
- 1 tbsp. cooking wine, adding depth and a hint of sweetness.
- 1 tbsp. hoisin sauce, for a rich, savory-sweet glaze.
- 1 tbsp. peanut butter, lending a creamy, nutty flavor.
- 1 tsp. low-sodium soy sauce, for that essential umami.
- 1 tsp. sriracha, adding a fiery spice.
- Season with salt, to enhance all the flavors.

Directions:

1. In a bowl, whisk together soy sauce, hoisin, cooking wine, sriracha, peanut butter, and water chestnuts until you have a smooth sauce.
2. Heat a skillet over medium heat. Begin by sautéing onions until they become translucent.
3. Add the garlic and ginger, stirring for a moment before adding the ground chicken. Season with a pinch of salt. Cook until the chicken is thoroughly browned.
4. Pour the sauce mixture into the skillet with the chicken, stirring well to ensure the chicken is evenly coated.
5. To assemble, lay out the butter lettuce leaves. Spoon the chicken mixture into the center of each leaf. Top with cucumber slices and a sprinkle of scallions.
6. Serve these flavorful wraps as a light yet satisfying meal, perfect for a nutritious lunch or dinner.

Nutrition Per Serving:

120 Kcal | Sodium 320 mg | Protein 14 g | Carbs 10 g | Fat 4 g | Potassium: 230 mg

Part 3: Soups & Salads

1. Exotic Spiced Chicken Soup

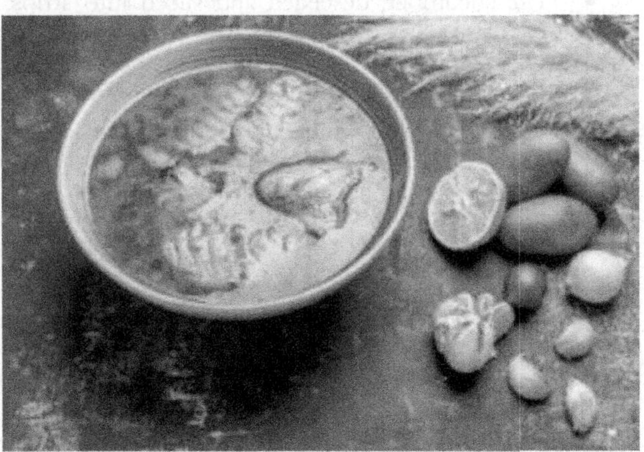

Skill Level: ★★☆☆☆

Prep Duration: 30 mins

Cook Duration: 1 hr 30 mins

Yield: 4 servings

Ingredients:

- 1 chicken breasts, boneless & skinless, prepared to enrich the soup with high-quality protein.
- 1 petite onion, finely chopped, to add a subtle, sweet flavor.
- 1/2 can (7.5 oz.) kidney beans, rinsed, to introduce fiber and texture.
- 14 oz. of crushed tomatoes with green chilis, for a zesty tomato base.
- 3.5 oz. pure tomato puree, to deepen the soup's rich tomato essence.
- 1/2 cup icy sweet corn, adding sweetness and crunch.
- 1/2 sachet of taco seasoning mix, infusing the soup with a vibrant array of spices.
- 1/2 can (7.5 oz.) pinto beans, thoroughly rinsed, for additional protein and body.
- 1/3 cup of fresh water, ensuring the perfect soup consistency.
- 1 tbsp. spice mix with red chili & coriander, for an aromatic kick.

Directions:

1. In a slow cooker, combine the chicken breasts, diced onion, kidney beans, tomatoes with green chilis, tomato puree, sweet corn, taco seasoning, pinto beans, water, and the spice mix. Stir well to ensure all ingredients are evenly distributed.
2. Cover with the slow cooker lid and set to high for a 3-hour cook for a richer flavor and tender chicken. Alternatively, for a gentler cooking process, set to low for 6 hours.
3. Once cooked, remove the chicken, shred it into thin strands using two forks, then return the shredded chicken to the pot. Stir well to mix the chicken back into the soup.
4. Serve the soup hot, allowing the blend of spices, tender chicken, and vegetables to comfort and delight with every spoonful.

Nutrition Per Serving:

155 Kcal | Sodium 120 mg | Protein 14 g | Carbs 20 g | Fat 1.5 g | Potassium: 450 mg

2. Herb and Citrus Egg Salad

Skill Level: ★★☆☆☆

Prep Duration: 30 mins

Cook Duration: 1 hr 30 mins

Yield: 2 servings

Ingredients:

- 4 eggs, boiled and segmented, forming the protein-rich base of the salad.
- 1/2 cup diced celery stalks, adding a crunchy, fresh texture.
- 1.5 tsp. pressed lemon, infusing the dish with a bright, citrusy tang.
- 1 tbsp. minced dill fronds, offering a fresh, herbaceous note.
- 1 tbsp. pickled capers, for a briny depth without the liquid.
- 1.5 tbsp. grainy mustard, contributing a tangy complexity.
- 1 tbsp. olive oil, to smooth and enrich the dressing.
- 1/4 tsp. ground garlic seasoning, for a mild, aromatic warmth.
- Salt crystals, fine-tuned to taste, enhancing the overall flavors.

- 1/4 tsp. freshly ground pepper, adding a spicy kick.

Directions:

1. In a mixing bowl, gently combine the finely chopped egg whites, capers, and celery, creating a textured salad base.
2. In another bowl, mash the egg yolks until they reach a creamy consistency. Whisk in the lemon juice, mustard, and olive oil, adjusting the dressing's thickness if necessary with a little more oil.
3. Stir in the garlic seasoning, salt, and pepper to the yolk mixture, ensuring the seasoning is evenly distributed.
4. Carefully fold the caper and celery mixture into the seasoned yolks, integrating all the elements without losing the lightness of the whipped yolks.
5. Serve this delightful mixture chilled, allowing the flavors to meld together harmoniously.

Nutrition Per Serving:

150 Kcal | Sodium 200 mg | Protein 9 g | Carbs 5 g | Fat 11 g | Potassium: 300 mg

3. Creamy Squash Soup Fusion

Skill Level: ★★☆☆☆

Prep Duration: 30 mins

Cook Duration: 1 hr 30 mins

Yield: 4 servings

Ingredients:

- 1/2 onion half, finely sliced, providing a savory sweetness to the soup.
- 2 pressed garlic cloves, adding depth with their robust flavor.
- 4 cups natural almond broth, for a nutty base that's both light and flavorful.
- 1 lb. butternut pumpkin (squash), diced, the star of the soup for its sweet, nutty taste.
- 1 tsp. virgin olive oil, for sautéing and enriching the flavors.
- 1 scoop powdered protein, neutral flavor, to increase the soup's protein content without altering its taste.
- 1 tsp. freshly grated ginger, introducing a spicy kick that complements the squash beautifully.
- Season with salt crystals and freshly milled pepper to taste, enhancing all the natural flavors.

Directions:

1. In a large pot, heat the olive oil over medium heat. Add the onion slices, cooking until translucent. Incorporate the garlic and ginger, sautéing briefly to release their aromas.
2. Add the diced butternut squash to the pot, followed by the almond broth. Season with salt and pepper. Bring the mixture to a gentle boil, then lower the heat and let it simmer until the squash is tender.
3. Use an immersion blender to puree the soup directly in the pot until it reaches a creamy consistency. If the soup is still hot (above 140°F), allow it to cool slightly before stirring in the protein powder to prevent clumping.
4. Once the protein powder is fully integrated and the soup is creamy, reheat gently if needed. Adjust the seasoning as desired.
5. Serve the soup hot, relishing the creamy texture and complex blend of flavors.

Nutrition Per Serving:

150 Kcal | Sodium 20 mg | Protein 12 g | Carbs 15 g | Fat 2 g | Potassium: 200 mg

4. Nourishing Greens and Sausage Broth

Skill Level: ★★☆☆☆

Prep Duration: 30 mins

Cook Duration: 1 hr 30 mins

Yield: 4 servings

Ingredients:

- 1 tsp. crushed garlic, for a bold, aromatic foundation.
- 1 red onions, sliced, adding a sweet depth.
- 1 cluster of kale leaves, stem removed and chopped, for a nutrient-rich addition.
- 6 oz. poultry sausage, sliced, introducing a savory protein element.
- 1/4 tsp. assorted spices (paprika, pepper flakes, garlic salt), for a flavorful kick.

- 1/2 can (7 oz) of navy beans, rinsed, to add fiber and texture.
- 1/2 can (5.5 oz) preserved tomatoes with green chilis, for a tangy spice.
- 4 cups chicken essence, creating a rich broth base.
- 1 bay leaf, to infuse the soup with aromatic flavors.
- 1/2 tsp. ground onion seasoning, for an extra layer of flavor.

Directions:

1. In an automated pressure cooker, combine the garlic, red onions, kale leaves, poultry sausage, assorted spices, navy beans, tomatoes with green chilis, chicken essence, bay leaf, and ground onion seasoning. Ensure all ingredients are evenly mixed for uniform flavor distribution.
2. Secure the lid and set the pressure cooker to high for a 10-minute cooking cycle. This quick, high-pressure cooking method allows the flavors to meld beautifully while tenderizing the ingredients.
3. Once the cooking cycle is complete, carefully release the steam according to the pressure cooker's instructions. Open the lid once it's safe to do so.
4. Stir the broth well, ensuring the kale and sausage are well incorporated. The soup should be hearty and vibrant with the greens slightly wilted but still tender.
5. Serve the broth hot, ladled into bowls. This soup combines the hearty, comforting essence of sausage with the wholesome, leafy goodness of kale, enriched by a flavorful broth.

Nutrition Per Serving:

150 Kcal | Sodium 320 mg | Protein 12 g | Carbs 10 g | Fat 5 g | Potassium: 200 mg

5. Hearty Lentil and Bean Stew

Skill Level: ★★☆☆☆

Prep Duration: 30 mins

Cook Duration: 1 hr 30 mins

Yield: 4 servings

Ingredients:

- 1 garlic clove, mashed, to add a pungent, aromatic depth.
- 1/2 golden onion, diced, providing a sweet and savory base.
- 1 young carrots, finely diced, for a subtle sweetness and vibrant color.
- 1 tsp. virgin olive oil, for sautéing and enriching flavors.
- 1/2 cups uncooked lentils, chosen for their earthy flavor and hearty texture.
- 1/2 tsp. chili essence, to introduce a warm, spicy note.
- 1/2 tsp. cumin seeds, adding a slightly nutty, warm aroma.
- 1/2 can (8 oz.) preserved tomatoes, for a tangy richness.
- 2 cups veggie stock, creating a flavorful broth base.
- 1/4 tsp. kosher salt, to enhance all the stew's flavors.
- 1/4 tsp. blackened red pepper, for a smoky, spicy kick.
- 1/2 can (8 oz.) black beans, rinsed, adding protein and depth to the stew.

Directions:

1. Begin by warming the olive oil in a large pot over medium heat. Add the mashed garlic to infuse the oil with flavor, followed by the diced onions and carrots. Sauté until the onions become translucent and the carrots start to soften.
2. Stir in the uncooked lentils, ensuring they're well coated in the oil and vegetable mixture. Sprinkle in the cumin seeds, chili essence, and blackened red pepper, stirring to distribute the spices evenly.

3. Pour in the preserved tomatoes and veggie stock, stirring to combine all the ingredients. Add kosher salt to taste.
4. Bring the mixture to a boil, then reduce the heat and let it simmer covered for about 30 minutes, or until the lentils and carrots are tender and the flavors have melded together.
5. Add the rinsed black beans to the pot, stirring them into the stew. Allow the stew to simmer for an additional 10 minutes, letting the beans heat through and the flavors to deepen.
6. Once cooked, adjust the seasoning if necessary, and serve the stew hot, garnished with fresh herbs or a dollop of sour cream for an added layer of flavor.

Nutrition Per Serving:

150 Kcal | Sodium 150 mg | Protein 8 g | Carbs 18 g | Fat 1.5 g | Potassium: 300 mg

6. Mediterranean Bean Salad with a Twist

Skill Level: ★★☆☆☆

Prep Duration: 30 mins

Cook Duration: 0 mins

Yield: 4 servings

Ingredients:

For the Salad:

- 1/4 cup chopped fresh basil leaves, for a fragrant herbal touch.
- 1 oz. crumbled reduced-fat goat cheese, adding tangy creaminess.
- 1/4 cup sliced green onion, for a sharp, fresh bite.
- 1/2 (7.5 oz.) can of Cannellini beans, drained, offering a smooth, buttery texture.
- 1/3 cup chopped zucchini, for a crisp, green crunch.
- 1/2 (7.5 oz.) can of Pinto beans, drained, for a hearty, earthy base.

For the Dressing:

- 1 tbsp. orange juice, for a sweet citrus zest.
- 1/2 tbsp. maple syrup, adding natural sweetness.
- 1/4 tsp. dried basil, for aromatic depth.
- 1 tbsp extra-virgin olive oil, to bind and enrich the dressing.
- 1/4 tsp. each of pink Himalayan salt & cracked pepper, for seasoning.
- 1/4 tsp. onion powder, enhancing the savory notes.
- 1/4 tsp. fennel seed, for a slight anise-like undertone.

Directions:

1. Whisk together all the dressing ingredients in a bowl until thoroughly combined. This creates a balanced, flavorful foundation for the salad.
2. In a separate bowl, combine the salad components—fresh basil, goat cheese, green onion, Cannellini beans, zucchini, and Pinto beans.
3. Drizzle the prepared dressing over the salad, gently tossing to ensure everything is evenly coated. The dressing will infuse the salad with its vibrant flavors.
4. Refrigerate the salad for 45 minutes, allowing the flavors to meld and the salad to chill thoroughly.
5. Serve the salad plated, offering a refreshing and satisfying meal or side dish.

Nutrition Per Serving:

110 Kcal | 75 mg Sodium | 6 g Protein | 11 g Carbs | 2.5 g Fat | 160 mg Potassium

7. Colorful Bell Pepper and Yam Bisque

Skill Level: ★★☆☆☆

Prep Duration: 30 mins

Cook Duration: 35 mins

Yield: 4 servings

Ingredients:

- 1/4 onion, sliced, for a base of savory flavor.
- 1 tsp. chopped fresh rosemary, adding a fragrant, herbal touch.
- Seasoning mix to taste, for personalized flavor enhancement.
- 1/2 carrot, sliced, for sweetness and color.
- 2 mixed (red & yellow) bell peppers, chopped, for a vibrant, sweet base.

- 1/4 peeled yam, diced, for natural sweetness and creaminess.
- 1 tsp olive oil, for sautéing the vegetables.
- 1 leek, chopped, for a mild, onion-like flavor.
- 2 cups chicken broth, to create a rich, flavorful liquid base.

Directions:

1. Heat the sunflower oil in a large pot over medium heat. Stir-fry the onion, carrot, leeks, and fresh rosemary with your choice of seasoning mix for 5 minutes until slightly softened.
2. Add the chopped bell peppers to the pot, stirring for another 5 minutes to begin softening the peppers.
3. Pour in the chicken broth and add the diced yam. Bring the mixture to a boil, then reduce the heat and let it simmer for 25 minutes, allowing the vegetables to cook fully and the flavors to meld.
4. Once the vegetables are tender, blend the mixture until smooth. Taste and adjust the seasoning as needed for the perfect balance of flavors.
5. Serve the bisque warm, enjoying the rich blend of savory, sweet, and herbal notes in every spoonful.

Nutrition Per Serving:

95 Kcal | 115 mg Sodium | 1.5 g Protein | 11.5 g Carbs | 2.5 g Fat | 160 mg Potassium

8. Crisp Orchard Salmon Salad

Skill Level: ★★☆☆☆

Prep Duration: 30 mins

Cook Duration: 0 mins

Yield: 4 servings

Ingredients:

- 2 oz. of fresh green beans, bringing a vibrant crunch.
- Zest & juice of 1 orange, offering a citrusy burst.
- 3 radishes, quartered, for peppery sharpness.
- 1/2 tbsp. of sunflower seeds, adding a nutty finish.
- 1 broccoli stalks, transformed into long, elegant ribbons.
- 1 tbsp. of olive oil, for a smooth, rich dressing.
- 1 grilled trout fillets, flaked into tender pieces.
- 1/4 bunch of parsley, leaves gently torn, for freshness.
- 1 tbsp. of Greek yogurt, creating a creamy, tangy dressing base.
- 1 oz. of alfalfa sprouts, for a delicate, crisp texture.

Directions:

1. Use a slicer to create thin, long ribbons from the broccoli stalks, avoiding the seedy center. In a large bowl, combine these ribbons with the quartered radishes, crisp green beans, and elegant broccoli ribbons for a base of diverse textures.
2. In a separate bowl, whisk together the Greek yogurt, orange juice and zest, and olive oil until smooth. This blend forms a dressing that's both creamy and bursting with citrus notes.
3. Arrange the flaked grilled trout and alfalfa sprouts at the bottom of your serving dish, laying down a foundation of protein and greens.
4. Gently layer the mixed vegetables on top of the trout and sprouts, ensuring a harmonious blend of colors and textures.
5. Finish by sprinkling sunflower seeds over the salad, adding a satisfying crunch and a nutty flavor.

Nutrition Per Serving:

110 Kcal | 75 mg Sodium | 8 g Protein | 5 g Carbs | 7 g Fat | 120 mg Potassium

9. Zesty Avocado Tuna Salad

Skill Level: ★★☆☆☆

Prep Duration: 30 mins

Cook Duration: 0 mins

Yield: 2 servings

Ingredients:

- 1/2 ripe avocado, offering a creamy, rich base.
- 1/2 tsp. of lime zest, for a bright, citrusy punch.

- 1/4 cup diced bell pepper, adding crunch and color.
- 1/4 tsp. of seasoning mix, to enhance flavors.
- 1 tbsp. of fresh cilantro, chopped, for herby freshness.
- 1 packet (2.6 oz) of albacore tuna in sunflower oil, for lean protein.
- 1 tsp. of lime juice, to tie all the flavors together with acidity.

Directions:

1. In a mixing bowl, combine the avocado, lime zest, diced bell pepper, seasoning mix, fresh cilantro, and packets of albacore tuna.
2. Using a fork, gently mix the ingredients until well integrated, ensuring the avocado is evenly distributed throughout.
3. Refrigerate the mixture for 90 minutes to allow the flavors to meld and the salad to chill.
4. Once chilled, plate the avocado tuna salad and serve as a refreshing, nutrient-rich meal.

Nutrition Per Serving:

140 Kcal | 105 mg Sodium | 11 g Protein | 7 g Carbs | 10 g Fat | 410 mg Potassium

10. Savory Wild Mushroom Soup

Skill Level: ★★☆☆☆

Prep Duration: 30 mins

Cook Duration: 25 mins

Yield: 4 servings

Ingredients:

- 1 shallot, finely diced, for a mild, aromatic base.
- 2 cups of beef broth, creating a rich and flavorful foundation.
- 1 garlic clove, minced, adding a robust depth of flavor.
- 8 oz. of a mixed fungi assortment, diced, for earthy notes and texture.
- 1 sprig of rosemary, infusing the soup with its fragrant, piney essence.
- 1 tsp of olive oil, for sautéing and adding a hint of fruitiness.
- 1 tbsp. of reduced-fat sour cream, for a creamy, tangy finish.
- 1 tbsp. of cornstarch, to thicken the soup subtly.

Directions:

1. In a large saucepan, heat the olive oil over medium heat. Sauté the minced garlic and diced shallots for about 7 minutes, or until they become soft and translucent, setting the stage for a flavorful broth.
2. Add the diced fungi to the pan and continue to stir for 4 minutes, allowing the mushrooms to begin to release their moisture and absorb the flavors.
3. Sprinkle the cornstarch over the mushrooms, stirring well to integrate and prevent clumps, ensuring a smooth texture for the soup.
4. Pour in the beef broth and bring the mixture to a boil. Then, reduce the heat, add the rosemary sprig, and let the soup simmer for 12 minutes. This step allows the flavors to meld beautifully.
5. Remove the rosemary sprig, then use an immersion blender or stand blender to puree the soup until smooth. This creates a rich, velvety consistency.
6. Adjust the seasoning as needed, and serve the soup hot, garnished with a dollop of reduced-fat sour cream for a luxurious finish.

Nutrition Per Serving:

90 Kcal | 55 mg Sodium | 3 g Protein | 4 g Carbs | 7 g Fat | 130 mg Potassium

11. Savory Forest Mushroom Soup

Skill Level: ★★☆☆☆

Prep Duration: 30 mins

Cook Duration: 25 mins

Yield: 4 servings

Ingredients:

- 1 shallot, finely diced, for a subtle, sweet flavor base.
- 2 cups of rich beef broth, providing a deep, savory foundation.
- 1 clove of garlic, minced, for aromatic warmth.
- 8 oz. of a mixed variety of fungi, diced, to bring the earthy essence of the forest.
- 1 sprig of rosemary, for a hint of aromatic herbiness.

- 1 tbsp of olive oil, for sautéing and adding a silky mouthfeel.
- 1 tbsp. of reduced-fat sour cream, for a creamy, tangy finish.
- 1 tsp. of cornstarch, to thicken the broth subtly.

Directions:

1. In a medium saucepan, sauté the minced garlic and diced shallots in olive oil over medium heat until they become translucent and fragrant, about 7 minutes.
2. Stir in the mixed fungi and cook for an additional 4 minutes, allowing the mushrooms to soften and release their flavors.
3. Sprinkle in the cornstarch and mix well to ensure it's fully integrated with the vegetables, helping to thicken the broth.
4. Gradually pour in the beef broth, increase the heat to bring the mixture to a boil, then reduce the heat. Add the rosemary sprig for an infusion of herbaceous flavor, and let simmer for 12 minutes.
5. Remove the rosemary, then carefully blend the soup until smooth. Season to taste, and serve hot with a dollop of reduced-fat sour cream for a creamy contrast.

Nutrition Per Serving:

80 Kcal | Sodium 55 mg | Protein 3 g | Carbs 4 g | Fat 6 g | Potassium: 100 mg

12. Velvety Broccoli Cheddar Soup

Skill Level: ★★☆☆☆

Prep Duration: 30 mins

Cook Duration: 1 hr 30 mins

Yield: 4 servings

Ingredients:

- 2 cups of broccoli florets, the star of the soup, offering a lush green hue and loads of nutrients.
- 1/4 tsp. of onion powder, adding depth and a hint of sweetness without the need for chopping.
- 1/4 cup of shredded carrots, for a touch of color and a natural sweetness.
- 2 cups of chicken broth, creating a rich, savory base that complements the broccoli beautifully.
- 1/4 tsp. of garlic powder, for a warm, aromatic flavor that infuses the soup.
- Salt & pepper, adjusted to taste, to perfectly season the dish.
- 1 cups of shredded cheddar cheese, reduced-fat to keep it lighter but still indulgently cheesy.
- 1/2 cup of low-fat heavy cream, to add luxurious creaminess without the guilt.
- 2 oz. of cream cheese, blending into the soup for extra silkiness and tang.

Directions:

1. Begin by combining the shredded carrots, broccoli florets, and chicken broth in a large, deep pot. Bring the mixture to a boil, then reduce the heat and let it simmer until the vegetables are tender and welcoming, inviting the spoon with every bite.
2. Stir in the onion and garlic powders to evenly distribute the flavors throughout the soup.
3. Gradually add the shredded cheddar, stirring continuously, ensuring it melts smoothly into the broth for that iconic, cheesy goodness.
4. Mix in the low-fat heavy cream, and cream cheese, watching as the soup transforms into a creamy delight. Adjust the seasoning with salt and pepper before turning off the heat.
5. Serve the soup hot, allowing each spoonful to be a warm embrace of creamy, cheesy, and veggie-packed goodness.

Nutrition Per Serving:

140 Kcal | Sodium 150 mg | Protein 7 g | Carbs 5 g | Fat 10 g | Potassium: 150 mg

13. Hearty Homestyle Beef Chili

Skill Level: ★★☆☆☆

Prep Duration: 30 mins

Cook Duration: 1 hr 30 mins

Yield: 4 serving

Ingredients:

- 1 sweet onion, finely diced, to lay a foundation of subtle sweetness.
- 3 stalks of celery, chopped, for a crisp, fresh texture.

- 2 ¼ tsp. dried oregano, adding a layer of earthy, herbal notes.
- 4 cloves of garlic, minced, for a bold, aromatic flavor.
- 2 ½ tbsp. chili powder, for that quintessential deep, smoky chili taste.
- 4 strips of bacon, chopped, to introduce a salty, savory crunch.
- 3 bell peppers, assorted colors, diced, to brighten the dish with sweet, vibrant flavors.
- 2.2 lbs. of ground beef, lean yet rich, providing the chili's hearty protein base.
- 1 (32 oz.) can of diced fire-roasted tomatoes, to infuse the chili with a smoky tang.
- Salt & pepper, adjusted to taste, for perfect seasoning.
- 2 ¼ tbsp. smoked paprika, for an additional layer of smokiness and warmth.
- 2 ½ tsp. ground cumin, lending an earthy spice that complements the beef beautifully.
- 2 ½ cups of low-sodium chicken broth, to bring all the ingredients together into a comforting stew.

Directions:

1. Begin by frying the bacon in a large skillet until crisp. Remove the bacon and set it aside, leaving behind a bit of rendered fat for flavor.
2. In the same skillet, add the diced peppers, onion, and celery. Sauté these vegetables until they are soft and translucent, enveloping the kitchen in their enticing aroma.
3. Add the ground beef to the skillet, breaking it apart with a spoon. Cook until the beef is thoroughly browned, ensuring it's fully incorporated with the vegetables.
4. Stir in the minced garlic, chili powder, smoked paprika, ground cumin, and dried oregano, letting the spices toast slightly and release their full spectrum of flavors.
5. Pour in the low-sodium chicken broth and the diced fire-roasted tomatoes. Bring the mixture to a simmer, then reduce the heat and allow it to cook gently for about 20 minutes, letting the flavors meld and deepen.
6. Serve the chili hot, garnished with the crisp bacon and your choice of toppings, inviting a comforting and satisfying meal experience.

Nutrition Per Serving:

450 Kcal | 750 mg Sodium | 30 g Protein | 10 g Carbs | 29 g Fat | 700 mg Potassium

14. Golden Roasted Cauliflower Soup

Skill Level: ★★☆☆☆

Prep Duration: 30 mins

Cook Duration: 1 hr 30 mins

Yield: 4 servings

Ingredients:

- 1 tbsp. ground cumin, for a warm, earthy spice that complements the cauliflower.
- 4 cloves of garlic, minced, infusing the soup with its aromatic essence.
- 1 large head of cauliflower, segmented, the star vegetable that offers texture and depth.
- 4 cups (32 oz.) of chicken stock, providing a rich, savory base to carry the flavors.
- 5 sprigs of thyme, lending a subtle, herbaceous aroma.
- 3 tbsp. olive oil, for roasting and sautéing, enhancing the soup's richness.
- 1 large onion, chopped, adding a foundational layer of sweet and savory notes.
- 1 bunch of fresh parsley, minced, for a fresh, bright finish.
- 2 sticks of celery, chopped, contributing a slight crunch and vegetal flavor.
- ½ cup (4 oz.) of low-fat cream, introducing a silky, indulgent texture without the heaviness.

Directions:

1. Begin by preheating your oven to 425°F (220°C). This high temperature is perfect for roasting, bringing out the natural sweetness of the cauliflower.
2. In a mixing bowl, toss the cauliflower segments with 1 ½ tbsp. of olive oil, fresh thyme leaves stripped from their sprigs, and ground cumin until evenly coated. Spread this mixture on a

baking tray in a single layer, ensuring each piece has room to caramelize.

3. Roast the cauliflower for 20 minutes, or until golden and tender. The edges should be slightly crisp, indicating it's perfectly done.
4. While the cauliflower roasts, heat the remaining olive oil in a large soup pot over medium heat. Add the chopped celery and onion, sautéing until they turn golden and aromatic. Stir in the minced garlic, being careful not to let it burn.
5. Add the roasted cauliflower to the pot with the sautéed onion, celery, and garlic. Pour in the chicken stock, bringing the mixture to a gentle simmer. Allow the flavors to meld together, simmering for an additional blend of time.
6. Once the vegetables are fully tender, remove the pot from the heat. Using an immersion blender, or in batches with a stand blender, purée the soup until smooth. Stir in the low-fat cream, warming through without bringing to a boil, to maintain its velvety texture.
7. Season the soup to taste with salt and pepper. Serve hot, garnished with a sprinkle of fresh minced parsley for a pop of color and freshness.

Nutrition Per Serving:

220 Kcal | Sodium 400 mg | Protein 6 g | Carbs 12 g | Fat 16 g | Potassium: 480 mg

15. Zesty Pork and Hominy Stew

Skill Level: ★★☆☆☆

Prep Duration: 30 mins

Cook Duration: 1 hr 30 mins

Yield: 4 servings

Ingredients:

- 1.5 lbs. of boneless pork shoulder, diced into bite-sized pieces, for a tender, flavorful protein base.
- 5 tbsp. of canola oil, chosen for its neutral flavor and high smoke point, perfect for browning meat.
- 3 ripe tomatoes, deseeded and chopped, adding a fresh, juicy component.
- 3 jalapeno peppers, deseeded and minced, for a controlled spicy kick.
- 6 cups of chicken broth, creating a savory liquid foundation for the stew.
- 1 can (15 oz.) of hominy, rinsed, to bring in a unique texture and slightly nutty flavor.
- 5 scallions, sliced, for a mild oniony crunch.
- 0.6 lb. of Andouille sausage, grilled and diced, infusing the stew with smoky, spicy undertones.
- 2 tbsp. of chili powder, to deepen the stew's complexity with smoky heat.
- 1 large onion, chopped, for savory depth and sweetness.
- 1 tbsp. of ground cumin, adding a warm, earthy spice.
- 1 cup of fresh cilantro, finely chopped, for a burst of herbal brightness.
- 1 tsp. of cayenne pepper, to dial up the heat for those who crave a spicy challenge.
- 3 cloves of garlic, minced, enriching the stew with aromatic flavor.
- 1 tsp. of coarsely ground black pepper, for a sharp, spicy note.

Directions:

1. In a large skillet over medium heat, heat the canola oil. Add the diced pork shoulder and grilled Andouille sausage, browning them evenly to lock in flavors.
2. Once browned, transfer the pork and sausage to a large stew pot. This will be the vessel where all the ingredients come together to create something truly special.
3. To the pot, add the chopped tomatoes, minced jalapeno peppers, sliced scallions, and minced garlic. Pour in the chicken broth and bring the mixture to a simmer, allowing the flavors to start marrying.
4. Stir in the rinsed hominy, chili powder, ground cumin, cayenne pepper, and black pepper. The spices will gradually infuse the broth with their vibrant flavors and aromas.
5. Let the stew simmer for an extended period, around 1 hour and 30 minutes, stirring occasionally. This slow cooking process tenderizes the pork, melds the flavors, and thickens the stew into a heartwarming dish.

6. Once the stew is ready, adjust the seasoning to taste. Serve hot, garnished with a generous sprinkle of fresh cilantro, adding a final layer of fresh, clean flavor to contrast the stew's richness.

Nutrition Per Serving:

350 Kcal | Sodium 890 mg | Protein 25 g | Carbs 15 g | Fat 20 g | Potassium: 450 mg

Part 4: Fish & Seafood Recipes

1. Parmesan-Herb Tuna Patties

Skill Level: ★★☆☆☆

Prep Duration: 30 mins

Cook Duration: 25-30 mins

Yield: 9 patties (1 serving= 1patty)

Ingredients:

- 4 cans of Tuna in water (4.5 oz. each), drained, for a light, protein-rich base.
- 3 large eggs, to bind the ingredients together.
- Green onions, finely sliced, for a fresh, oniony crunch.
- 1 1/4 cups of low-fat Parmesan cheese, finely grated, for a cheesy flavor without the extra fat.

Directions:

1. In a large mixing bowl, thoroughly combine the drained tuna, eggs, sliced green onions, and grated Parmesan cheese. This mixture should have a consistent texture for forming cakes.
2. With clean hands, form the mixture into 9 evenly-sized cakes, compacting them so they hold together during baking.
3. Place the tuna cakes on a baking tray lined with baking paper to prevent sticking.
4. Preheat your oven to 350°F (175°C). Once preheated, bake the tuna cakes for 25-30 minutes, or until they turn golden and slightly crispy on the outside.
5. Allow the tuna cakes to cool for a few minutes before serving. This resting period helps them set and makes them easier to handle.

Nutrition Per Serving(1 patty):

130 Kcal | 310 mg Sodium | 18 g Protein | 1.5 g Carbs | 6 g Fat | 250 mg Potassium

2. Spicy Shrimp and Sausage over Squash Noodles

Skill Level: ★★☆☆☆

Prep Duration: 30 mins

Cook Duration: 30 mins

Yield: 2 serving

Ingredients:

- 0.6 lb. cooked and deveined Shrimp, for a seafood delight.
- 4 oz. Andouille sausage, cut into pieces, for smoky depth.
- 1 medium tomato, seedless and chopped, for fresh sweetness.
- 13 oz. Butternut squash noodles, as a low-carb, nutrient-rich base.
- 1.5 tsp. Cajun spices (no salt added), for that spicy kick.
- 2 tsp. Tomato concentrate, to enrich the sauce.
- Seasoning, to taste, ensuring the dish is perfectly flavored.
- 1 fresh jalapeno pepper, seedless and sliced, for an extra zing.

Directions:

1. Begin by heating a large skillet over medium-high heat. Add the sausage pieces and fry until they're nicely browned, bringing out their flavor.
2. Add the cooked shrimp to the skillet, warming them through. Then, remove the shrimp and sausage from the skillet and set aside on a plate.
3. In the same skillet, add the chopped tomato. Introduce a splash of water and the tomato concentrate, stirring until the mixture is homogeneous.
4. Toss in the butternut squash noodles, cooking and stirring occasionally until they reach a tender consistency.

5. Return the shrimp and sausage back to the skillet, mixing well to ensure the flavors meld together beautifully.
6. Serve the dish garnished with slices of jalapeno pepper, adding a final touch of heat.

Nutrition Per Serving:

320 Kcal | 670 mg Sodium | 25 g Protein | 10 g Carbs | 18 g Fat | 550 mg Potassium

3. Mustard-Glazed Salmon Filet

Skill Level: ★★☆☆☆

Prep Duration: 30 mins

Cook Duration: 10 mins

Yield: 1 serving

Ingredients:

- 6 oz. wild salmon, for a rich, omega-3 packed main.
- 1 ½ tbsp. Dijon mustard, for a tangy glaze.
- A pinch each of dry parsley, kosher salt, and freshly ground black pepper, for seasoning.
- A small pinch of cayenne spice, for a gentle heat.
- 1/4 tsp. garlic powder, for aromatic depth.

Directions:

1. Begin by preheating your oven to 400°F (204°C), setting the stage for a quick, high-heat cook.
2. Cut the salmon into two equal pieces to ensure even cooking. Generously brush each piece with Dijon mustard, covering all sides.
3. Evenly sprinkle the seasoned salmon with parsley, salt, black pepper, cayenne, and garlic powder, creating a flavorful crust.
4. Heat a skillet over a medium flame. Once hot, sear the salmon for approximately 2 minutes on each side, developing a delicious crust.
5. Transfer the skillet directly to the preheated oven. Bake for about 3 minutes, or just until the salmon is cooked to your preference. This method ensures the salmon remains moist and flavorful.
6. Serve the salmon immediately, enjoying the harmonious blend of mustard tang and spices that beautifully complement the fish's natural flavors.

Nutrition Per Serving:

250 Kcal | 450 mg Sodium | 28 g Protein | 1 g Carbs | 14 g Fat | 450 mg Potassium

4. Zesty Shrimp and Vegetable Foil Packets

Skill Level: ★★☆☆☆ Prep

Duration: 30 mins

Cook Duration: 15-20 mins

Yield: 2 serving

Ingredients:

- 1.1 pounds of large shrimp, peeled and deveined, offering a lean, flavorful protein.
- 3.5 cups of chopped zucchini, for a low-calorie, nutrient-rich addition.
- 3 garlic cloves, crushed, to infuse a robust flavor.
- 2 tbsp. of extra-virgin olive oil, for healthy fats and moisture.
- Freshly ground salt and pepper, to taste, ensuring perfect seasoning.
- 2 tbsp. of fresh cilantro, minced, for a burst of freshness and color.
- 1 tsp. of smoked paprika, adding a subtle, smoky flavor depth.

Directions:

1. In a large mixing bowl, thoroughly combine the shrimp, chopped zucchini, crushed garlic, extra-virgin olive oil, minced cilantro, and smoked paprika. Season with salt and pepper to taste, ensuring each ingredient is well-coated.
2. Cut large pieces of aluminum foil, sufficient to hold the mixture and fold into packets. Distribute the shrimp and vegetable mixture evenly among the foil pieces.
3. Carefully fold the foil around the mixture to form sealed packets, making sure no juices can leak out.
4. Preheat your oven to 400°F (204°C). Place the sealed packets on a baking tray and bake for about 15-20 minutes, or until the shrimp are pink and fully cooked.

5. Carefully open the foil packets (watch for steam), and serve the shrimp and vegetables immediately, enjoying the melded flavors and tender textures.

Nutrition Per Serving:

350 Kcal | 800 mg Sodium | 35 g Protein | 8 g Carbs | 20 g Fat | 800 mg Potassium

5. Lemon-Caper Tilapia Piccata

Skill Level: ★★☆☆☆

Prep Duration: 30 mins

Cook Duration: 20 mins

Yield: 2 serving

Ingredients:

- 2 tilapia fillets, offering a mild, versatile base.
- 1 tbsp. of olive oil, for searing and flavor.
- 1 tbsp. all-purpose flour, to thicken the sauce subtly.
- 1 tsp. minced garlic, for aromatic depth.
- 1 tbsp. capers, adding a briny pop.
- 1/4 cup of champagne vinegar, for a sophisticated acid component.
- Juice of 1 lemons (about 2 tbps), providing fresh, citrus notes.
- 1 tbsp. of butter, to enrich the sauce.
- Seasoning to taste, ensuring perfect flavor balance.

Directions:

1. Heat the olive oil in a skillet over medium heat. Lightly season the tilapia fillets with your preferred seasoning and sear for about 2 minutes on one side until golden. Then, gently transfer them to a plate.
2. In the same skillet, melt the butter. Stir in the flour and cook for a minute, just until the raw flour taste is gone, creating a roux.
3. Slowly whisk in the champagne vinegar and lemon juice, integrating them into the roux to form a smooth sauce.
4. Add the capers to the sauce, letting them simmer for a minute to infuse their flavor.
5. Taste and adjust the seasoning of the sauce as needed. Gently pour the lemon-caper sauce over the seared tilapia.
6. Serve the tilapia immediately, garnished with a slice of lemon or a sprinkle of fresh herbs if desired.

Nutrition Per Serving:

200 Kcal | 350 mg Sodium | 20 g Protein | 3 g Carbs | 11 g Fat | 400 mg Potassium

6. Grilled Shrimp Wraps with Zesty Cream Sauce

Skill Level: ★★☆☆☆

Prep Duration: 30 mins

Cook Duration: 10 mins

Yield: 4 serving

Ingredients:

For the Zesty Cream Sauce:

- ¼ cup of Greek yogurt, for a tangy, creamy base.
- ¼ tsp. of paprika, for a smoky flavor.
- 1 fresh tomato, chopped, for juicy sweetness.
- ¼ cup of cream cheese, for richness.
- Juice from half a lemon, adding a bright citrus note.

For the Tortillas:

- 2 ¼ cups of shredded lettuce, for crunch and freshness.
- 4 wheat tortillas, serving as the versatile wrap.
- 1 tsp. of vegetable oil, for grilling.
- 1 lb. of shrimp, cleaned & deveined, as the protein star.
- ½ tsp. of coriander powder, for a hint of spice.
- Garnish with fresh parsley & green onions, for flavor and color.

Directions:

1. For the sauce: In a bowl, mix Greek yogurt, cream cheese, paprika, and lemon juice. Stir until smooth. Fold in the shredded lettuce and chopped tomato, blending gently.
2. Prepare the shrimp by marinating it with coriander powder and vegetable oil. Ensure each shrimp is evenly coated.

3. Heat a grill pan over medium heat. Grill the shrimps for about 5 minutes on each side, or until they're pink and slightly charred.
4. Assemble the wraps: Lay out the wheat tortillas, and place a portion of the grilled shrimp in the center of each tortilla.
5. Drizzle the zesty cream sauce over the shrimp, then garnish with parsley and green onions.
6. Roll up the tortillas to encase the filling neatly, and serve immediately.

Nutrition Per Serving:

250 Kcal | 400 mg Sodium | 25 g Protein | 20 g Carbs | 10 g Fat | 450 mg Potassium

7. Smoky Salmon & Crunchy Veggie Grain Bowl

Skill Level: ★★☆☆☆

Prep Duration: 30 mins

Cook Duration: 10 mins

Yield: 2 serving

Ingredients:

- 1 cucumber, diced, for a refreshing crunch.
- ½ cup sliced carrots, adding a sweet, earthy note.
- Your choice of dressing, to enhance flavors.
- 1 red bell pepper, diced, for color and sweetness.
- 2 cups cooked vegetable rice (or 1 packets if using pre-packaged), for a hearty, healthy base.
- 1 cup chopped purple cabbage, for texture and vibrant color.
- 1 cup smoked salmon chunks, providing rich, smoky protein.

Directions:

1. Begin by preheating your oven to 425°F (220°C). Lightly grease a baking tray and evenly spread the vegetable rice across it.
2. Cook the vegetable rice in the oven for about 7 minutes, stirring occasionally to ensure even baking.
3. Once baked, distribute the vegetable rice among serving bowls.
4. Add the diced cucumber, sliced carrots, diced red bell pepper, chopped purple cabbage, and chunks of smoked salmon atop the vegetable rice.
5. Drizzle your chosen dressing over the bowl contents, then gently toss everything together to evenly coat the ingredients.
6. Serve the bowls immediately, enjoying a symphony of flavors and textures that make for a satisfying, nutrient-packed meal.

Nutrition Per Serving:

350 Kcal | 450 mg Sodium | 20 g Protein | 40 g Carbs | 15 g Fat | 500 mg Potassium

8. Herb-Infused Baked Tilapia with Vegetables

Skill Level: ★★☆☆☆

Prep Duration: 30 mins

Cook Duration: 15 mins

Yield: 2 serving

Ingredients:

- 3 cups of zucchini, diced for a tender, mild base.
- 1 tbsp. garlic paste, adding a robust flavor.
- ¼ tsp. chili powder, for a gentle kick.
- 1 ½ cups of radish, sliced for crunch and peppery notes.
- 2 tilapia fillets (about 6 oz each), lean and perfect for a light, satisfying meal.
- 2 tbsp. sunflower oil, ensuring moist, flavorful fish.
- 1 yellow bell pepper, sliced for a sweet, colorful addition.
- Salt & black pepper to taste, for perfect seasoning.
- 1 tbsp. chopped dill, for a fresh, herbaceous finish.
- ¼ tsp. garlic powder, reinforcing the garlic flavor.

Directions:

1. Begin by preheating your oven to 400°F (200°C), setting up for a quick, efficient bake.

2. Toss the diced zucchini, sliced radish, and yellow bell pepper with 2 tablespoons of sunflower oil. Season with salt and black pepper, then spread out on a baking tray, ready for the oven.
3. In a small bowl, blend the remaining oil with garlic powder, chili powder, and additional salt and pepper. Coat each tilapia steak evenly in this mixture, preparing them for a flavorful roast.
4. Arrange the seasoned fish on top of the prepped veggies on the tray, creating an all-in-one meal setup.
5. Bake for about 14 minutes, just until the fish is flaky and vegetables are tender.
6. Sprinkle the baked dish with fresh dill for a burst of flavor right before serving.

Nutrition Per Serving:

250 Kcal | 300 mg Sodium | 30 g Protein | 10 g Carbs | 12 g Fat | 700 mg Potassium

9. Citrus-Infused Salmon with a Sweet Glaze

Skill Level: ★★☆☆☆

Prep Duration: 30 mins

Cook Duration: 15 mins

Yield: 2 serving

Ingredients:

- 8.5 oz. wild salmon, for a hearty, omega-rich main.
- 1 ½ tbsp. Dijon mustard, offering a tangy glaze.
- A dash each of turmeric powder and paprika, for color and a mild kick.
- ¼ cup orange juice and 2 tbsp. lime juice, for a citrusy marinade.
- 1 tbsp. white sugar, adding sweetness to balance the citrus.
- 2 tsp. orange zest, for an aromatic citrus boost.
- ½ tsp. salt, to enhance all flavors.
- ¼ tsp. nutmeg, for a hint of warming spice.

Directions:

1. Preheat your oven to 400°F (200°C) to get it ready for the salmon.
2. Slice the salmon into two pieces if needed and generously brush each with Dijon mustard.
3. Create a marinade by mixing the orange and lime juices, then let the salmon soak in this citrus blend for about an hour, turning occasionally to ensure even flavoring. Drain and discard the marinade afterward.
4. Combine the spices—turmeric, paprika, orange zest, nutmeg, and salt—and thoroughly coat the salmon pieces with this mixture.
5. Grease a baking tray, place the seasoned salmon on it, and bake for about 13 minutes or until the salmon is perfectly cooked to your liking.
6. Serve the salmon hot, basking in its sweet and citrus-infused glaze.

Nutrition Per Serving:

Kcal 280 | Sodium 410 mg | Protein 25 g | Carbs 12 g | Fat 12 g | Potassium 450 mg

10. Mozzarella-Crusted Baked Tilapia

Skill Level: ★★☆☆☆

Prep Duration: 30 mins

Cook Duration: 10 mins

Yield: 2 serving

Ingredients:

- 2 tilapia fillets, offering a mild, versatile base.
- 2 tbsp unsalted butter, for richness and moisture.
- 1 ½ tbsp. mayonnaise, creating a creamy adhesive for the crust.
- ¼ cup grated mozzarella, for gooey, cheesy goodness.
- ¼ tsp. white pepper, adding subtle, sharp heat.
- 1 tbsp. apple cider vinegar, to tenderize and infuse tang.
- ¼ tsp. dried oregano, for herbal notes.
- A dash each of garlic salt and onion salt, for flavor depth.

Directions:

1. Start by activating the broiler on your oven, preparing it for a quick, intense cook.
2. In a mixing bowl, thoroughly combine unsalted butter, mayonnaise, grated mozzarella, white

pepper, apple cider vinegar, dried oregano, garlic salt, and onion salt. This mixture will serve as the flavorful crust for the tilapia.

3. Lightly grease a baking pan and arrange the tilapia fillets on it, ensuring they have space between them for even cooking.
4. Broil the tilapia for about 3 minutes on each side, just until they begin to flake and turn opaque—a sign they're almost done.
5. Remove the pan from the oven briefly to spread the cheese mixture over each fillet, then return to the broiler for an additional 2 minutes, or until the topping is golden and bubbly.
6. Serve the tilapia hot, with its mozzarella crust beautifully bronzed and flavors melded together.

Nutrition Per Serving:

320 Kcal | 350 mg Sodium | 30 g Protein | 2 g Carbs | 20 g Fat | 450 mg Potassium

11. Citrus Herb Halibut Delight

Skill Level: ★★☆☆☆

Prep Duration: 20 mins

Cook Duration: 15 mins

Yield: 3 serving

Ingredients:

- 3 halibut fillets (about 5 oz. each), for a lean and flavorful base.
- 1/3 cup Chardonnay, to add depth and a slight fruity undertone.
- 2 tsp. chopped garlic, for a bold flavor kick.
- ¼ cup finely chopped fresh parsley, for freshness and color.
- Juice from 1.5 limes, offering a zesty citrus burst.
- 1.5 tbsp. extra virgin olive oil, for moisture and richness.

Directions:

1. Preheat your oven to 410°F (210°C) and lightly grease a medium-sized baking tray for easy fish removal.
2. In a bowl, whisk together the Chardonnay, lime juice, extra virgin olive oil, chopped garlic, and parsley to create a flavorful marinade.
3. Place the halibut fillets on the prepared baking tray and generously brush them with the marinade, ensuring each piece is well-coated.
4. Bake the marinated halibut for 14-17 minutes in the preheated oven. The exact time may vary depending on the thickness of the fillets, so adjust accordingly.
5. Once the halibut is cooked through and flaky, remove from the oven and let it rest for a minute before serving, allowing the flavors to meld together perfectly.

Nutrition Per Serving:

250 Kcal | 120 mg Sodium | 25 g Protein | 4 g Carbs | 12 g Fat | 650 mg Potassium

12. Nut-Crusted Baked Fish with Herbs

Skill Level: ★★☆☆☆

Prep Duration: 20 mins

Cook Duration: 25 mins

Yield: 2 serving

Ingredients:

- 1.2 pounds fresh white fish, a perfect canvas for flavors.
- 1/3 cup ground flaxseed, for a nutty, crunchy crust.
- 1/3 cup ground hazelnuts, adding depth and richness.
- 3 tbsp. mayonnaise, to help the crust adhere and add moisture.
- ½ cup grated low-fat cheddar, for cheesy goodness without the guilt.
- 2 tsp. chopped garlic, for a pungent kick.
- ¼ tsp. white pepper and ½ tsp. of a garlic and ½ tsp. onion powder mix, for subtle spice and flavor layers.
- ¼ tsp. dried oregano, for a hint of earthiness.
- 2 eggs, beaten, to bind the coating.
- ¼ tsp. baking powder, to help the crust puff slightly.

Directions:

1. Preheat your oven to 445°F (230°C) and drop a small dollop of butter onto a baking tray to melt as the oven warms.

2. In one bowl, whisk the eggs until frothy. In another bowl, combine ground flaxseed, ground hazelnuts, grated low-fat cheddar, garlic, white pepper, garlic and onion powder mix, dried oregano, and baking powder.
3. Dip each fish piece first into the dry mixture, ensuring it's fully coated, then into the beaten eggs, and back into the dry mix for a second coating.
4. Place the coated fish strips on the buttered baking tray. Bake in the preheated oven for 12 minutes. Mist the fish lightly with oil, flip, and bake for another 7-12 minutes until golden.
5. For an extra crunch, broil for 3 minutes. Serve the fish warm, directly from the oven.

Nutrition Per Serving:

480 Kcal | 640 mg Sodium | 38 g Protein | 12 g Carbs | 34 g Fat | 580 mg Potassium

13. Flavorful Herb-Encrusted Low-Carb Fish

Skill Level: ★★☆☆☆

Prep Duration: 18 mins

Cook Duration: 28 mins

Yield: 2 serving

Ingredients:

- Seasoning salt and freshly ground black pepper, to taste, for perfect seasoning.
- 16 oz. fresh fish fillets (such as tilapia, cod, or halibut), as a lean, protein-rich base.
- 1.5 tsp. herb seafood seasoning, infusing the dish with aromatic flavors.
- A light sprinkle of cayenne pepper, adding a gentle heat.

Directions:

1. Start by preheating your oven to 380°F (193°C), ensuring it's ready for baking.
2. Prepare a baking sheet by lining it with foil for easy cleanup. Place the fish fillets on the sheet.
3. Sprinkle the fish with seasoning salt, black pepper, herb seafood seasoning, and a touch of cayenne pepper to create a flavorful crust.
4. Bake in the preheated oven for about 27 minutes, or until the fish is cooked through and flakes easily with a fork. The precise time may vary based on the thickness of the fillets.

Nutrition Per Serving:

180 Kcal | Sodium 200 mg | Protein 36 g | Carbs 0 g | Fat 4 g | Potassium: 600 mg

14. Lemon-Infused Salmon and Green Beans

Skill Level: ★★☆☆☆

Prep Duration: 17 mins

Cook Duration: 12 mins

Yield: 2 serving

Ingredients:

- 2 tbsp vegan butter, for a rich, creamy base.
- Salt & freshly ground pepper to taste, for seasoning.
- 10 oz. fresh green beans, cleaned & trimmed, for a crisp, healthy side.
- 12 oz. boneless salmon fillets, for a heart-healthy main.
- Juice from 1 lemon, adding a fresh, citrusy zing.

Directions:

1. Melt the vegan butter in a large skillet over medium heat, creating a flavorful foundation for the dish.
2. Place the salmon fillets and green beans in the skillet. Cook the salmon for about 4 minutes on each side until golden and nearly cooked through. Toss the green beans occasionally to ensure even cooking and flavor infusion.
3. Season the salmon and green beans generously with salt and freshly ground pepper, tailoring the dish to your taste preferences.
4. Just before serving, drizzle the fresh lemon juice over the salmon and green beans, enhancing the flavors with a bright citrus note.
5. Serve warm, offering a beautifully balanced meal that's both satisfying and health-conscious.

Nutrition Per Serving:

Kcal 320 | Sodium 180 mg | Protein 28 g | Carbs 10 g | Fat 20 g | Potassium 700 mg

15. Garlic-Thyme Cod with Goat Cheese

Skill Level: ★★☆☆☆

Prep Duration: 12 mins

Cook Duration: 14 mins

Yield: 2 serving

Ingredients:

- 2 cod portions (4.5 oz. each), offering a mild and flaky base.
- 1.5 crushed garlic cloves, adding a rich, aromatic flavor.
- 3 tomatoes, segmented for a fresh, acidic balance.
- 1.5 tsp. olive oil, to sauté and enhance flavors.
- 8 oz. fresh spinach, for a healthy, vibrant side.
- 2 oz. creamy goat's cheese, for a tangy, rich topping.

Directions:

1. Preheat your oven to 395°F (202°C), readying it for baking.
2. In a pan, sauté the crushed garlic with a splash of water to soften. Add the spinach and cook until wilted, dividing it into two oven-safe dishes.
3. Place the cod fillets on top of the spinach beds. Layer each fillet with goat's cheese and tomato segments.
4. Bake in the oven for about 12 minutes, or until the fish is cooked through and the cheese is slightly melted.
5. Serve hot, enjoying the harmonious blend of flavors from the garlic and thyme-infused cod, complemented by the creamy goat's cheese and the fresh, juicy tomatoes.

Nutrition Per Serving:

250 Kcal | 150 mg Sodium | 28 g Protein | 6 g Carbs | 12 g Fat | 700 mg Potassium

8-Week Meal Plan

Over the next 8 weeks, let's embark on a culinary journey tailored to your bariatric diet, exploring a variety of flavors and textures designed to meet your nutritional needs while keeping your taste buds delighted. Here's your revamped meal plan based on the recipes provided:

Week 1 - Stage 1: Clear Liquids
Day 1-7:

- **Morning:** Healing Herbal Broth
- **Afternoon:** Country Vegetable Essence
- **Evening:** Strawberry Bliss Jelly
- **Optional:** Rich Beef Bone Broth

Week 2 - Stage 2: Full Liquids and Pureed Foods
Day 8-14:

- **Morning:** Vanilla Custard, Berry Melon Refreshment
- **Afternoon:** Creamy Butternut Squash and Ginger Soup, Carrot and Ginger Cream Soup
- **Evening:** Savory Vegetable & Egg Tart, Mango & Avocado Salsa
- **Snack:** Chocolate Protein Shake

Week 3 - Stage 2: Continued
Day 15-21:

- **Morning:** Lemon Berry Energy Smoothie, Green Vitality Smoothie
- **Afternoon:** Creamy Yogurt & Garlic Shrimp, Berry Protein Jello Cups
- **Evening:** Creamy Parmesan Cauliflower & Bean Purée, Root Vegetable Harmony Puree
- **Snack:** Cherry-Chocolate Smoothie Delight

Week 4 - Stage 3: Semi-Solid/Soft Foods
Day 22-28:

- **Morning:** Ricotta-Laced Scrambled Eggs, Banana-Spinach Energy Smoothie
- **Afternoon:** Citrus-Infused Chicken with Spinach, Savory Spinach & Feta Herb Pie
- **Evening:** Mediterranean Chicken and Vegetable Harmony, BBQ-Flavored Turkey Muffin Loaves
- **Snack:** Pumpkin Spice Protein Smoothie

Week 5 - Stage 3: Continued
Day 29-35:

- **Morning:** Herbaceous Chicken with Tomato-Spinach Ragout, Baked Ricotta Herb Casserole
- **Afternoon:** Caprese-Inspired Chicken Fillets, Savory Pork & Bean Soup with a Yogurt Twist
- **Evening:** Asian-Inspired Chicken Lettuce Wraps, Creamy Chicken and Cauliflower Casserole
- **Snack:** Divine Chicken Salad Spread

Week 6 - Stage 4: Transition to Regular Diet (Appetizers & Sides)
Day 36-42:

- **Morning:** Caprese Salad Bites, Artichoke & Zucchini Parmesan Rounds
- **Afternoon:** Chickpea & Crispy Bacon Deviled Eggs, Baked Crispy Zucchini Chips
- **Evening:** Easy Tomato and Basil Soup, Savory Pinto Bean Dip
- **Snack:** Almond Mozzarella Pretzel Bites

Week 7 - Stage 4: Meat & Poultry Recipes
Day 43-49:

- **Morning:** High-Protein Chicken Salad, Holiday Protein Eggnog
- **Afternoon:** Robust Veggie & Bean Chili, Savory Turkey Taco Casserole
- **Evening:** Kale-Infused Turkey Bites, Spicy Chicken Cheese Bites
- **Snack:** Citrus Herb Halibut Delight

Week 8 - Stage 4: Fish & Seafood Recipes
Day 50-56:

- **Morning:** Almond-Crusted Fish with Tomato Basil Topping, Citrus-Infused Salmon with a Sweet Glaze
- **Afternoon:** Zesty Shrimp and Vegetable Foil Packets, Parmesan-Herb Tuna Patties
- **Evening:** Herb-Infused Baked Tilapia with Vegetables, Mustard-Glazed Salmon Filet
- **Snack:** Nut-Crusted Baked Fish with Herbs

Remember, this meal plan serves as a guide to help you navigate your post-bariatric surgery diet with ease. It's important to listen to your body and consult with your healthcare provider to adjust the plan according to your specific needs. Enjoy the flavors and the journey towards a healthier you!

Conclusion

The complexities of our digestive system play a pivotal role in nutrient processing within our bodies. Exploring the dynamics and advantages of gastric bypass surgery reveals its profound alteration of this system. This operation is far from a minor adjustment; it's a substantial modification designed to aid weight loss by reducing stomach volume and rerouting the digestive tract.

Gastric bypass surgery primarily diminishes the stomach's size, leading to earlier satiety with less food, thereby reducing caloric consumption. Additionally, it modifies nutrient absorption by bypassing certain intestinal areas, further cutting down calorie uptake. This dual approach significantly impacts food intake and absorption.

While any surgical intervention, including bariatric surgery, carries risks, the procedures maintain high success rates, especially when performed in reputable, certified medical facilities. These centers employ a multidisciplinary team, from surgeons to dietitians, ensuring comprehensive patient care across all fronts, both physical and psychological.

The importance of aftercare cannot be overstated. Successful outcomes hinge not only on the surgery but also on a patient's adherence to a new lifestyle. This includes new eating habits, regular exercise, and routine supplementation. Such dedication, alongside continuous healthcare monitoring, helps in early detection and management of possible complications or deficiencies.

For those contemplating this life-changing surgery, it's essential to consider all facets. Consulting with medical professionals to weigh the surgery's risks against the health consequences of ongoing obesity is crucial. The aim extends beyond mere weight loss to enhancing overall life quality.

In essence, while gastric bypass surgery provides a viable option for battling obesity, its true effectiveness is realized when combined with a comprehensive, lifelong health commitment. Success lies in the synergy of medical intervention and personal dedication to adopting healthier nutritional habits, staying active, and maintaining mental well-being. The procedure is merely a stepping stone; the journey to better health is a shared effort between medical support and individual commitment.

Index

SUPPLEMENTARY CONTENTS

Unlock Hidden Insights!

Scan the QR code below to access three exclusive enhancements that complement your culinary journey through the **"Gastric Bypass Cookbook"**. These handpicked resources provide essential tips, tricks, and dietary advice to maximize the benefits of your post-surgery diet. Dive deeper into the art and science of nutrition, empowering yourself to make informed and delicious food choices.

If you encounter any issues or have feedback to share, feel free to reach out directly at **megan.rush@mindsparkpressltd.com**. Your insights and experiences are vital in our mission to offer the best possible guidance and support to our readers. Let the culinary discoveries begin!

YOUR FEEDBACK MATTERS

Dear Reader,

Thank you for choosing to embark on this transformative journey with the "**Gastric Bypass Cookbook**". I sincerely hope that the recipes and insights offered in this book will guide and support you as you navigate the post-surgery culinary landscape.

The decision to undergo gastric bypass is a significant one, and adopting the right dietary habits post-surgery is crucial for success. This cookbook aims to provide delicious and nutritious recipes that cater to the unique needs of individuals post-gastric bypass.

If you've found the recipes helpful and enjoyed the culinary delights, **I would be grateful if you could share your experiences by leaving a review on Amazon**. Your feedback not only helps me fine-tune the content but also assists others in choosing resources that suit their needs. By sharing your story, you become an inspiration for many who are on a similar journey, helping to foster a community of support and understanding.

For further insights, recipe suggestions, or to share your own success stories, feel free to connect at **megan.rush@mindsparkpressltd.com**. Your active participation and feedback will shape the future editions of this cookbook, ensuring that it remains relevant and valuable for those who need it the most.

Thank you for letting me be a part of your post-surgery journey. Here's to health, happiness, and a lifetime of culinary joy!

With sincere appreciation,

Megan Rush

Made in the USA
Columbia, SC
17 January 2025